A. C. Becker's

SPECKLED TROUT:

How, When, & Where

A. C. Becker's SPECKLED TROUT:

How, When, & Where

By A. C. Becker, Jr.

BOZKABOOKS

P.O. Box 271369
Houston, Texas 77277-1369
713/666-8602

Published by
BOZKABOOKS

Second printing, March, 1989

Cover illustration by Mark Mantell

Layout and cover design by John Hillenbrand

ISBN:0-929980-01-8

Library of Congress Catalog Card Number: 88-92412

This one is for my son, Carl
who accompanied me on many
speckled trout fishing trips;
and to his wife, Sawrie
and their sons,
Ryan Robert
and
Derek Carl.

CONTENTS

FOREWORD

Coastal fishermen, through necessity more than anything else, are gamblers at heart. They have to be.

"Guaranteed" fishing trips simply don't exist.

They gamble on the weather. They gamble on the word of the bait camp operator. They gamble on where to fish, what time to do it, and what type of bait to use. And some, primarily those who have been at it for a long time, win more often than they lose.

There's no better way to learn the art of speckled trout fishing than from a veteran, someone who has devoted years of trial-and-error tactics toward the goal of consistent success. Trouble is, these "old salts" are about as secretive as gourmet chefs guarding award-winning recipes.

That's not the case with A.C. Becker, Jr. I learned that in a hurry when I became editor of Texas Fisherman magazine back in 1980.

A.C. began his "Coastal Fisherman" column with that publication during its first year, in 1973. From day one, he has made himself available to the fishing public, listing his phone number in each and every issue.

I found it more than a little amazing that he would subject himself to such a massive flood of phone calls. So I asked him why he did it.

"Ideas," he said. "That's how I get my story ideas. I find out what's on the minds of saltwater fishermen; then I research it and write about it."

That willingness to share, coupled with decades of writing and angling experience, has made A.C. the dean of Gulf Coast outdoor writers. Fishing for speckled trout and other saltwater species is experiencing a tremendous surge in popularity, and his knowledge has never been more in demand.

A third-generation Galvestonian and second-generation newspaper man, A.C. worked as sports and outdoors editor of The Galveston Daily News for 44 years. He sold his first fishing article to Field & Stream magazine in 1946.

A.C. attended Galveston schools, and is a journalism graduate of the University of Texas at Austin. He's a veteran of special writing seminars held at Columbia University in New York, the American Press Institute, Sam Houston State University and Arlington State University.

Since that first article, he has had fishing or waterfowl-hunting features published in 26 national and regional magazines. During that period, he has also written outdoor features for the Dallas Morning News, Houston Post, Fort Worth Star-Telegram, New Orleans Times Picayune, Oklahoma City Daily Oklahoman, Tulsa World, Washington Post and Texas Press Association.

He's a charter member, former vice-president and four-time director of the Texas Outdoor Writers Association, and has been a member of the Outdoor Writers Association of America since 1959.

This book is his tenth title, and is the first one A.C. has written in over 10 years. Though he still writes some material for the paper, he retired from the Galveston Daily News in May, 1987. A year later, I left Texas Fisherman to begin publishing books and instructional videotapes, and the first project was one that A.C. and I had been conceptualizing for years ... the book you're holding in your hands.

The general topic of fishing for speckled trout has been covered numerous times in outdoor magazines, but until this title hit the presses, there was no single reference book on the market dedicated solely to the subject of locating and landing these beautiful game fish.

No, it won't guarantee you success every time you hit the water. There are too many variables involved to ever assume that fishing for specks, or any other species, is going to be a sure-fire proposition.

But it will increase your odds, no matter if you're a first-time trout-chaser or a seasoned master of the sport.

Matter of fact, I'd be willing to bet on it.

Larry Bozka   Houston, Texas

INTRODUCTION

Biologists call the fish Cynoscion nebulosus. Its proper common name is spotted seatrout, although the fish isn't really a trout in the true meaning of the word. The people who fish for it call it a speckled trout, but after they've caught a few, they refer to it with more familiarity as either a trout or a speck...sort of like the name David becomes Dave, Charles becomes Chuck, ad infini-

tum as one becomes more familiar with the subject. Depending upon the part of the coast where the fish is found, it has been, and occasionally still is, called a spotted weakfish, spotted squeteague or saltwater trout.

Regardless what the fish is called, it's the No. 1 game fish found in the inshore waters of the northern Gulf of Mexico... the surf, jetties, bays, and tidal bayous and rivers.

The information and fishing techniques presented in this book are the result of 50 years of fishing coastal waters of the southern United States and 40 years of writing about fishing. Some of the facts presented I learned first-hand, occasionally on a trial-and-error basis. Much of the information, certainly at least 80 percent, was gathered from the fishing experts in the field: guides, boat captains and deckhands, bait dealers, lure and tackle manufacturers, skilled sports anglers, commercial fishermen, marine biologists, and just plain old salts who knew no other way of life.

I know I must have annoyed many of them with my frequent "how, when, and where" questions. I've often been accused of spending more time taking notes than fishing. But that was the way I was trained when I roamed through the School of Journalism at the University of Texas in Austin.

I've written a great many articles on specks and speckled trout fishing. Not one was really complete, because with the printing of each, there came new bits of information.

It will be the same with this book. The day after it is printed, new information, techniques, tackle and skills will undoubtedly unfold in the continuing saga of the speckled trout.

This is only proper. We should look upon fishing for speckled trout as a developing story. Fish with an open mind, for this is the only way we can absorb new information and ideas.

The next step, then, is to go out and apply the points. That's the purpose of this book: to get you, the reader, to look upon speckled trout as an exciting fish to catch...and then accept the challenge.

A. C. Becker, Jr.   Galveston, Texas

1.
THE SPECKLED TROUT

The speckled trout, Cynoscion nebulosus, is by far the most popular species of the Cynoscion clan. That status can be attributed to both the fighting ability and table quality of this beautiful sport fish. Its proper name is "spotted seatrout." (photo by Larry Bozka)

I developed a yen for catching speckled trout, and a distaste for eating them, back in the mid-1930s. That's when my father initiated me into what is today called "sport fishing." At the time, however, it was more "necessity fishing," since we were smack-dab in the middle of the Great Depression. It was a time when very few people fished for recreation or sport; they fished to put food on the table.

And that, I'm sure, is what caused my distaste for eating fish, a distaste that lasted until after the conclusion of World War II. I suspect a lot of other youngsters of my generation wrinkled their noses, too, when it came to eating fish.

Remember, I'm speaking here of the days before portable ice chests and home freezers were available. Thus, a day's catch was suspended on a stringer in the water. The popular way of stringing was to run the line through the fish's mouth and out of the gills, or vice versa. Either way, it was a sure way to kill your catch.

And fish, being quite tender, were quick to deteriorate. The meat didn't spoil to the point of being unfit to eat, but just enough to acquire a fishy smell that wasn't very appetizing, especially to youngsters. It was, in fact, too much like cod liver oil.

Although it took me years to overcome the taste-bud block, the excitement of catching specks never waned.

THE FAMILY

The speckled trout isn't a trout in the true definition of the word, but a member of the croaker (Sciaenidae) family. A true trout is a member of the salmon family, a species that moves back and forth between salt and fresh water, spawning only in fresh water. The speckled trout, on the other hand, is strictly a saltwater fish.

The speckled trout is specifically catalogued as Cynoscion nebulosus. The accepted common name is spotted seatrout, but along most of the coast of the northern Gulf of Mexico, it is "provincialized" to speckled trout, or "speck." In fact, on some parts of the coast, the natives insist on spelling it "spec" instead of "speck."

Three of the four members of the Cynoscion genus are common in northern Gulf coastal waters. The most popular is C. nebulosus, the speckled trout. The other two are the silver seatrout (C. nothus) and the sand seatrout (C. arenarius). In the eyes of speckled trout enthusiasts, the silver seatrout and sand seatrout, respectively called gulf trout and sand trout, are just poor cousins of the regal speck.

The fourth member of the Cynoscion genus is the weakfish (C. regalis). This fish, which grows larger than the speckled trout, is basically an Atlantic coast fish, rarely straying into the Gulf of Mexico.

Of the three species of the Cynoscion genus in the Gulf of Mexico, the gulf trout and sand trout are more plentiful than the speck, and they are easier to catch. But based on its size, fighting ability, beauty and table quality, the speckled trout stands head and shoulders above the gulf trout and sand trout.

Anyone can catch a few speckled trout, even a trophy mount, but it takes an expert to catch them consistently. Consequently, a person who cares to specialize in catching specks must have a thorough knowledge of the fish, its characteristics and its habits.

DESCRIPTION, CHARACTERISTICS

Without question, the speckled trout is the most beautifully marked member of the Cynoscion clan. The torpedo-shaped body has a darkish-gray back that flashes powder-blue or iridescent reflection. Very young specks have backs that appear velvet-black. The upper portion of the fish (above the median line and extending over the dorsal fin and tail) is marked with round black spots. These appear velvety on young fish: and while the spots tend to fade as these fish age, they do not vanish altogether, as do the markings on various other species of fish. The speck's lower sides and belly are silvery. There is a yellowish-orange tinge around the mouths of large female specks. Old salts call these "yellow-mouth sows."

The fish's scales are small, delicate and easy to remove. The tail and fins have soft rays. The soft fins and squarish tail indicate the fish is more "homebody" than migratory.

The fish can open its mouth very wide, but the membrane around it is quite delicate and tears easily. The fish has two pronounced canine teeth at the front tip of its upper jaw. The remainder of the teeth in both the upper and lower jaws are small.

SPAWNING PERIOD

Speckled trout spawning is directly linked to light and the length of daylight. There are several major hatches during the year, the peak occurring in April and May. A second major spawning period of short duration occurs in September, with continuous small spawns through the summer.

The start of the peak spawns depends upon the water temperature. It begins when the temperature reaches 68 degrees.

Rainfall and freshwater runoff can influence the quality of the hatch, especially if the salinity of nursery waters is markedly increased or decreased.

Spawning takes place in the vicinity of grass stands and saltgrass marshes. The grass offers the fry cover and food. The fish remain close to the grass until they are about an inch long, beginning to venture more and more to open water as they grow.

Speckled trout have been known to spawn when they were as small as eight inches. More realistically, the average spawn start for male specks is when they are about 10 inches long. Females start spawning when they are about 12 inches long.

Most Gulf coast states have minimum keeper lengths on specks. The purpose is to get the fish through at least one spawning period before it grows to keeper size. Since these minimum keeper lengths are not standard across the coast, it behooves fishermen to check game digests for regulations in the state in which they fish.

RATE OF GROWTH

The growth rate of specks depends upon the food supply. The young grow fast, spending only 12 to 15 days hidden on flooded grass flats. After that first two weeks, the growth rate slows and is greatly influenced by the weather. The young suffer during periods of drought, when the saline content of the water may soar, and during heavy rain and freshwater runoff when they may be swept out of the grass. And if that's not enough, there are the large female sows themselves. If enough natural fodder isn't available, mama specks will turn right around and devour their young.

Female specks grow faster than males, live longer and reach a larger size. Few males live beyond five years. Based on growth rates, some female specks caught have been calculated to be 13 to 14 years of age.

Some years ago, the Texas Parks and Wildlife Department made a study of trout growth rates in the Laguna Madre. The study showed male specks, ages one through seven years, reached the following lengths in inches: 5-1/2, 8, 10-1/2, 14, 15-1/2, 16 and

Migrations of speckled trout rarely exceed more than 25 or 30 miles from their spawning area. Nonetheless, a few tagged specimens have ventured as far as 70 miles from the site at which they were tagged. Water temperature and salinity greatly influence migrations. (Photo by A.C. Becker, Jr.)

16-1/2. Female trout for the same ages reached the following lengths in inches: 5-1/2, 9, 12, 14-1/2, 16-1/2, 18-1/2 and 21.

Biologists, putting together all known facts gathered in Gulf coast studies, note the following length averages in inches for ages one through six: 8, 11, 14, 17, 20 and 23. Growth rates are not uniform for all Gulf coast states, the habitat, food supply and temperature of the water probably accounting for the differences.

TRAVEL IN SCHOOLS

Speckled trout feeding habits and characteristics undergo changes with age and growth.

During the first year of life, specks dine almost exclusively on shrimp. Locate concentrations of small grass shrimp and you'll find schools of young speckled trout.

Young trout travel in schools, sometimes numbering many hundreds of fish. These fish are generally uniform in size. This would tend to indicate members of the school all came from the same hatch. These juvenile specks spend most of their time in shallow bays and in the general vicinity of grass stands and reefs. They tend to move into very shallow water and small bayous at night, but move back to deeper water as day breaks and the light increases.

As speckled trout grow in size, the schools become smaller When the fish are one-pounders, schools are likely to contain hundreds of fish. By the time the fish are three- to four-pounders, the schools dwindle to several dozen fish. Trophy-size specks going six pounds or more are loners or travel in pods of three or four fish.

Instead of almost exclusively following shrimp, as is the case with school-size specks, big trophy-class trout dine mostly on bait fish such as mullet, mud minnows, pinfish and small croakers. Biologists report as well that while big trout dine heavily and may only feed once a day, the school-size fish feed several times a day, gorging themselves to the point of regurgitation, and then continue their feeding binges.

Big sow trout frequently turn on smaller specks of six to eight inches. Some years ago, a study was made of the stomach contents of large specks in fish markets. The study revealed that over half of the fish examined contained the remains of small trout.

MIGRATION OF TROUT

Speckled trout are migratory only in the sense that they move back and forth between shallow and deep water. Unlike some species of fish, speckled trout do not move north and south with the seasons.

When specks are young, they roam mainly in the general vicinity of their spawning area, close to grass stands and saltgrass marshes. According to tagging studies, small one- to two-year-old fish remain within several miles of where they were spawned. As they grow older, they roam more, but even so the migrations are generally less than 25 or 30 miles of the spawning area. There are exceptions, of course, as a few tagged fish have been recovered as far as 70 miles from the tagging site.

The big sows are fairly predictable in that they will move onto the flats in the vicinity of marshes, first in the spring and then a second time in the early fall. Both of these moves coincide with major spawning runs.

Water temperature and saline content influence migrations. Specks move onto the flats when the temperature is mild or moderate, meaning a range of 68 to 78 degrees. When the water temperature falls under 60 or climbs above 85 degrees, they make a definite retreat to deeper water.

Specks move back and forth between the bays of the Gulf of

Mexico, but seldom more than several hundred yards out into the Gulf. The exception is along jetties, where they will move out as far as the end of jetties, although they invariably move along close to the structure.

EFFECTS OF WEATHER

The temperature of the water and saline content are influenced by the weather. Specks move toward the Gulf in the summer when bay water temperatures soar during drought periods, and again when heavy rains and freshwater runoff "sweeten" bays by causing the saline content to drop.

Barometric pressure falls when weather fronts move into an area. Speckled trout, like most species of fish, tend to feed with almost reckless abandon in the high-pressure period that precedes an approaching weather front. This may be Mother Nature's way of fattening up the species to survive the lean days when the front rolls in.

It's pretty much the same with the passage of tropical disturbances that may occur during the summer months. As the storm approaches, it's extremely difficult to find trout. It's a different story the day after the passage of the blow. The fish may be scattered, but when you find them, they feed voraciously.

FOOD VALUE

The table quality of speckled trout depends upon the size of the fish and the care given it prior to preparation for the table.

Most fish eaters agree that specks between one and two pounds are the tastiest. The meat is firm, white, sweet and without a fishy flavor. The bigger the trout, the more coarse and less sweet the meat, which has an oily, fishy flavor, which many people find objectionable.

Specks five pounds or larger are almost always females, and therein lies clues as to how the fish is going to taste on the table. Specimens heavy with roe tend to be oily. The meat of speckled trout taken right after they spawn is generally soft and sometimes of poor texture.

CLEANING AND COOKING

How and when your fish is dressed has a lot to do with its palatability.

Small trout can be scaled, gutted, headed and cooked whole.

There is a lot of wasted meat in trying to fillet small trout. Deep frying is generally the best way to prepare the small fish.

Larger specks from about two pounds up can be filleted without having to scale or gut the fish. Making sure to use a very sharp knife, cut straight down just behind the head to the backbone. Then turn the knife and cut carefully toward the fish's tail. Stop short of completely severing the slab of meat from the fish. Flip the slab over and carefully cut between the meat and the skin. Repeat the procedure on the other side of the fish.

These fillets can be deep-fried or broiled in a lemon-butter mix. If you plan to bake the fish, be careful not to overcook or your meat will dry out and crumble.

Fish meat is much more tender than red meat. Hence, it need not be cooked as long. The meat of speckled trout is even more tender than that of most fish, so particular care must be taken to avoid overcooking it. When it's done, the meat will flake easily off the bone when touched with a fork. **BB**

2.
TACKLE
FOR SPECKLED
TROUT

Speckled trout, even the bigger "sows," can be taken on fairly light tackle. Note the seven-foot rod; the extra length serves both to further casting distance and to allow the angler more maneuverability. (photo by Larry Bozka)

I caught my first speckled trout in the early 1930s. Fishing for piggy perch at the time, I was using thread for line and a small safety pin for a hook. Many years later, I was fishing for bull redfish near the end of the Galveston South Jetty. I was using a stout Calcutta cane rod, a 5/0 reel and 40-pound-test line. I caught several large redfish and a speckled trout on the derrick rig that day.

The trout caught on the thread-and-bent-pin combo put up a heck of a fight, although it was only a scrawny half-pounder. The trout caught years later on the heavy gear weighed a little over four pounds, but it offered very little excitement on the heavy tackle.

These two incidents illustrate that speckled trout can be caught on all kinds of tackle, but if you want to enjoy catching them consistently, the tackle should be tailored to fit the fish. This is a tactic that applies to all species of fish.

Specks, even big sows weighing six or seven pounds or more, are light-tackle fish. If you want to enjoy the fight of the fish, you must go with light gear. Remember, the fish has a very tender mouth, and unless you cushion the shock when the fish strikes or makes a sudden run, the hook may tear out of the flesh. This is most likely to occur if heavy tackle is used.

The other side of the coin is equally bad. If the tackle is ultra-light, you might have to battle the fish a long time before it can be led to the landing net. In a long battle a hook can wear a hole in the tender flesh, and if the fish turns and runs toward you fast enough to put slack in the line, the hook can drop out ... and the fish has won its freedom. Then all you have left is talk about how "the big one got away." And you know how people take to those tales.

RODS AND REELS

The longer one fishes, the more one appreciates good tackle. Through more than 50 years of fishing, I have caught speckled trout on rods that ranged from homemade cane poles to today's sensitive graphite and boron rods.

The homemade cane poles were used back in the Great Depression Days when money was scarce and "plastic money" was not yet around. Then came my first split bamboo, again homemade, followed a few years later by the steel rod that resembles today's CB antennas. Next came solid fiberglass rods, followed by hollow fiberglass, and finally graphite, boron and combinations thereof.

Each new rod material was an improvement. Not only did I enjoy fishing more, but I enjoyed greater success with the increasingly sophisticated rods.

Pick a rod with medium-light to medium action in a length of six to seven feet. The length is important; if you fish from a boat, rod length acts as a lever and shock absorber to keep the fish from going under the boat or around the motor's lower unit. The length also gives the wade fisherman the advantage of distance when casting, and believe me ... distance is a must when fishing in shallow water.

Although some fishermen use rods with short handles or pistol grips, a better choice is the two-handed butt 10 to 12 inches long. This type of butt enables the user to make long casts. It also aids in making the rod a lever for controlling the direction in which a hooked fish swims.

My early baitcasting reels were "knuckle-busters" that lacked any kind of drag devices. Additionally, I didn't own a levelwind reel until after World War II. I had to use thumb and forefinger to guide line onto the reel spool as I was reeling in a fish.

Today's reels come in four types: conventional (baitcasting)

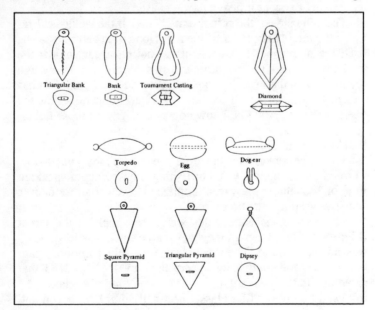

with revolving spool, open-face spinning, closed-face spincast and fly. All but the fly reel are used widely for speckled trout fishing. There are people who fish for specks with fly tackle, but this technique is used mostly in Florida waters. It is not that fly tackle is unsuitable; rather, it is highly specialized tackle that requires unusual skill to use properly and effectively, especially in saltwater where wind is often a major factor.

Whatever type of reel you use, it should be a size that matches the size and action of the rod. Open-face spinning and closed-face spincast reels are easiest to cast, with absolutely no backlashes. These reels, however, must be cleaned frequently when used in saltwater.

Most Gulf coast speckled trout anglers prefer the conventional reel with star drag and levelwind. These reels will stand the abuse of everyday fishing in saltwater with a minimum of care and repair. Yet along the Atlantic Coast, most anglers use spinning gear.

An important point to keep in mind when purchasing a reel is to buy a brand that is popular in the area where you do most of your fishing. Parts will wear out and occasionally reels will malfunction. It is important to get on-the-spot service, rather than

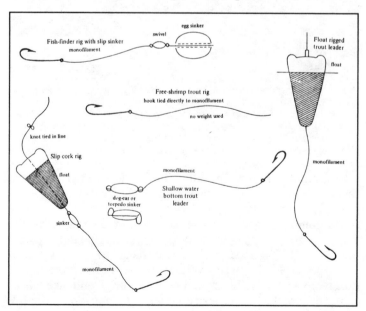

The "popping cork" is a standard item of tackle for the fisherman chasing speckled trout. The concave top of the float makes a chugging noise when popped via the rod. The use of these floats, in fact, eventually led to the development of long but stout "popping rods." These rods offer medium-action blanks designed to throw the corks and terminal tackle long distances while retaining the backbone to set a hook. (photo by Larry Bozka)

wait a month or so because the reel has to be returned to the factory. Unless you have spare equipment, you can miss a lot of good fishing this way.

In comparison with similar-size fish of other species, the speckled trout does not make long runs. A five-pound bonefish may peel off 50 yards of line before it changes directions. Not so with specks. Even a heavyweight sow won't run more than a dozen or so yards before changing directions. Don't take this as a negative for the fish. Instead of a couple of long runs, the speck will make a number of short ones, and it will fight right up until it is led into the landing net.

Even though the fish's runs are short, always keep your reel filled to capacity with line. This makes for easier casting, and in the case of conventional reels, a full spool lessens the probability of backlashes. Furthermore, the drag will operate more smoothly when line is being pulled from a near-full reel rather than a half- or quarter-filled spool.

FISHING LINES

Complement your rod and reel with the proper line. Although most trout caught by the average angler are under two pounds, it would be a mistake to use ultra-light line. Remember, you're fishing in waters than could yield a 20-pound redfish or a six- to seven-pound flounder.

Twelve- to 15-pound test-line is adequate for fishing speck waters. I have whipped king mackerel and jackfish as large as 40 pounds on 15-pound-test. It just takes time, and the fight is what makes fishing exciting.

If the line is too heavy for the rod and reel, distance is lost in the cast. Heavy line also deprives the angler of the "feel" he must have when the fish are only toying with the bait. I know some very good speck fishermen who switch to 10-pound-test line in the winter, so they can better "feel" the nibbling at the bait when fish are sluggish from the cold.

When I started fishing back in the 1930s, a fellow had a choice of linen, cotton or silk line. Each material required washing and drying after every trip if you wanted the line to last any length of time. Today, we have fine lines made of synthetics. It comes braided and in monofilament form. This line wears well, withstands the elements and given even cursory care, it will last several years.

Monofilament line comes in almost as many colors as are in the rainbow. I have a feeling that some of the gaudy orange, yellow and red lines are just as easy to see from the fish's viewpoint as from the fisherman's. Personally I prefer clear, mist-blue, mint-green or camouflage monofilament line. Each blends nicely with the water, and none stands out so as to spook fish when the water is gin-clear.

Monofilament line comes in many grades. Don't be misled by cut-rate prices; bargain-priced lines are often "seconds," or even "factory rejects" that are sold without a brand name. This line may be frayed, brittle, stiff and not uniform in either strength or diameter. Better to spend a few dollars more and buy line that will do a first-class job. Always keep in mind that record fish usually come along only once in a lifetime. Talking about the record that got away is less than a hollow victory.

Monofilament line spooled tightly on a reel has a tendency to take a set. This can be minimized by occasionally taking the line off the reel and stretching it for an hour or so. Do it in the shade, because direct sunlight can fade or discolor the line. Limpness can be restored to the line by removing the spool from the reel and soaking the spool and line overnight in a pot of fresh water.

SINKERS

The trout fisherman needs a variety of sinkers, but they should be in weights, sizes and shapes tailored to the fish and the fishing gear. The most common mistake is to go "overweight," meaning to use sinkers that are too heavy. The extra weight may be helpful in gaining a few extra yards on the cast, but the bigger splash caused by the heavier sinker when it hits the water may spook the fish. This can be a major problem on sand flats where the water is shallow. Furthermore, the extra weight can hamper the action of live bait, and when that happens, you simply defeat the purpose of using live bait.

There is no such thing as a universal sinker or weight that will serve all purposes. Therefore, buy an assortment of sinkers ranging from a quarter-ounce to half-ounce in the following styles: ring-eye or torpedo, dog-ear or pinch-on, rubber core, egg and oval. Also, get an assortment of split-shot ranging up to one-eighth of an ounce. Split-shot is a secondary weight often used eight to 10 inches above the live bait in order to prevent the bait from swimming to the surface. It is used in this fashion when the bait is fished under a float. If you cannot get egg or oval sinkers, worm sinkers will do almost as well.

A ring-eye or torpedo sinker with a swivel attached is excellent to use between the line and leader when strong currents are likely to spin the bait in such a manner that it would put a twist in the line.

FLOATS, POPPING CORKS

Except in the dead of winter or in deep water, a float is usually necessary in speckled trout fishing. This is especially true when fishing bays, where bait on the bottom is at the mercy of crabs and hardhead catfish. This can be a real problem when bottom fishing in warm weather.

The proper float to use is one specifically designed for speckled trout fishing. The float has a dished or concave top that makes a distinct "pop" on the surface of the water when the fishing rod is snapped up smartly. This float is called a "popping cork," and it originated many decades ago in Texas. The "pop" is much like the sound a large speck causes when it strikes at something near the surface. In effect, proper use of the popping cork is a way of calling fish. I have seen expert anglers use the technique to stir specks into feeding frenzies.

Another effective speck imitator that is fast gaining popularity is known as the "Mansfield Mauler." Developed by Port Mansfield fishing guide Bob Fuston, the wire-leadered orange bobber has become a favorite of fishermen on Texas' lower coast. Most often, the rig is fished above a lead-headed shrimp tail. When popped, the stiff wire leader causes the lure to hop, much like a shrimp kicking its tail. At the same time, rattles on both ends mimic the sound of a snapping shrimp.

Floats come weighted and unweighted. I prefer the weighted models because they eliminate the need of additional sinkers on the leader. Furthermore, I feel weighted floats make casting easier, in that there is less of a tendency for the hook and bait to flip back and tangle the leader or wrap around the line above the float.

Floats come in various colors: red, green, blue, yellow, orange and white. The white or white-topped floats are best for night fishing because they can be seen if there is just the faintest moonlight. White, however, is difficult to see during the daylight hours if there is enough wind to put a chop or whitecaps on the water.

SNAPS AND SWIVELS

There is no great need for snaps and swivels, but you should carry some in your tackle box for special situations. Neither snaps nor swivels should be used immediately between the hook and leader. Use of either simply adds extra weight that will only burden live bait. If the terminal rig is to be used as a fish-finder, then use a swivel 18 to 24 inches above the bait.

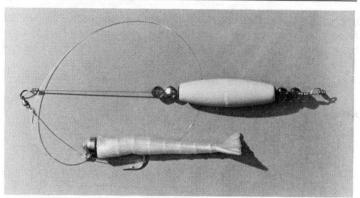

Developed by Port Mansfield fishing guide Bob Fuston, the "Mansfield Mauler" cork rig is fast becoming a favorite of Gulf Coast fishermen. Most often fished in tandem with a lead-headed shrimp tail, the beaded orange bobber does a convincing job of imitating a tail-snapping shrimp. (photo by Larry Bozka)

Use an egg, oval or worm sinker on the line above the swivel. This is a bottom rig that allows the live bait and current to pull out line through the slip-sinker. It proves a good terminal rig to use for fishing the jetties, on sand flats or in deep holes in the winter.

Do not use snaps or swivels with artificial lures unless the lures come so equipped. Many lures are delicately balanced, and when you use additional hardware,, you may spoil the action. This, however, is less of a problem in salt water than in fresh water, because saltwater lures are bigger and heavier.

TROUT LEADERS

There is really no need for special leader material for speckled trout rigs. Since the fish doesn't have razor-sharp teeth, you can forget about wire or cable leaders. If you do use some sort of wire leader you would only defeat the purpose of using live bait, because such a leader would be so stiff it would cancel out the action of the bait.

Monofilament will serve nicely as leader material. I let my monofilament fishing line itself serve as the leader by simply attaching the float or sinker on the line about two to three feet above the hook. When the fishing day is over, I cut off the part of the line that served as the leader and discard it. That way, I always have fresh line for a leader for the next fishing trip.

This trick serves another purpose, too: it uses up line and every so often, forces me to get new line. That way, I'm not going to get stuck with old line that becomes stiff with age or turns into tight coils like a wire spring.

HOOKS FOR SPECKS

The real business end of every fishing rig is the hook. Without it, you have no connecting link with the fish. Use good-quality hooks and carry a hone so you can keep hooks as sharp as needles. A hone or sandpaper can also be used to remove rust from hooks. If sharpening and cleaning hooks is too much of a chore, then simply get rid of them when they show signs of wear. New hooks don't cost that much, especially when it becomes a question of catching or losing fish.

Treble or gang hooks are the choice of most speckled trout anglers. A three-tined hook may sound unsportsmanlike to the purist, but anyone who has done a lot of trout fishing knows the need for three tines. The soft mouth of the fish makes maintaining a good connection a major task. When live bait is used, go with hooks in sizes 4, 6 and 8. They are small and light and will not interfere with the action of the bait. Use No. 6 and 8 treble hooks for fishing the bays. The No. 4 treble is a better choice for jetty waters where the trout are generally bigger and larger baits are used.

Speckled trout can open their mouths quite wide, certainly wide enough to take a 2/0 to 4/0 hook with ease. While this may be so, the weight and size of a large hook works against the fisherman not only by inhibiting live-bait action, but also by wearing a hole in the tender flesh of the fish's mouth. Then, with the least bit of slack in the line, the hook is likely to fall free, and there goes your fish ... maybe even a record one. And it all happened because the wrong hook was used.

So don't overlook the importance of hooks; the hook is to fishing what the rifle bullet is to deer hunting or the shotgun pellet is to bird and waterfowl hunting. **BB**

3.
NATURAL BAITS FOR SPECKLED TROUT

Live shrimp are unbeatable trout baits in terms of all-around effectiveness. Though they're relatively expensive and can be difficult to keep alive in hot weather, many will settle for nothing else. (photo by A.C. Becker, Jr.)

Shrimp and speckled trout go together like bread and butter or bacon and eggs. Locate where the shrimp are working, and the odds heavily favor finding speckled trout nearby.

This does not mean, however, that shrimp are the only creatures trout feed on. All you need do is cut open the specks you catch and note the stomach contents. In fact, examining stomach contents is a must if the fishing is slow. It can indicate a change in baits or in fishing techniques that could improve your catch.

A case in point happened to me some years ago before bag limits were imposed on the fish. My daughter Laura and I were wade fishing the beachfront at Galveston, using live shrimp under popping corks. The action was very slow for us, although we could see others who were using lures catching speckled trout on both sides of us.

We had two specks on our stringer. I cut them open and examined their stomach contents, and found the remains of small shiners. Laura and I immediately switched to spoons. She tied on a Mr. Champ, a small spoon that darts erratically when retrieved. I put on a Johnson Sprite spoon that was twice as large. She caught two trout on her next dozen casts. I drew blanks, but when I changed to a much smaller Johnson Sprite, I immediately started catching fish.

It was obvious we were in a school, and when we had about 10 fish on the stringer, I decided to do a little experimenting. I changed back to live shrimp, fishing them under a float as well as on the bottom. in the next half-hour, Laura caught something like five trout to my every one.

Usually, you catch the most trout on live shrimp. But this was different. The answer may have been in the size of the fish. All were three- to three-and-a-half-pound fish, well above the average size for specks. Biologists note that as specks grow larger, they are more inclined to augment their diet with small fish. In fact, several fisheries biologists have told me they believe more than half the diet of large speckled trout is made up of small fish.

But all speckled trout are not big. In fact, the majority are fish that weigh between a pound and a pound-and-a-half. These are the fish the average sport angler will encounter on a daily basis. Trout this size feed mostly on shrimp, so if one is to catch consistently, then shrimp make the best bait.

Speckled trout are fastidious eaters that feed on fresh bait, not garbage. Don't use bait that stinks or is ripe with age. Stink baits are for catfish, not speckled trout. It's interesting to note, however, that the speck's poorer relatives, gulf trout and sand trout, readily take dead shrimp.

LIVE SHRIMP

If you plan to fish for specks with natural bait, then the first choice should be live shrimp. This bait is unbeatable when it comes to fishing bay flats, around reefs and along the edges of grass stands and marshes. These are the areas where trout are likely to school in large numbers.

As far as some species of fish are concerned, the larger the bait, the bigger the fish that is likely to be caught. In the case of speckled trout, however, the bait must be tailored to the waters fished. Shrimp six and seven inches long make good bait for trout when the fish are uniformly large (three to four pounds), or when you are fishing jetty waters or in passes and channels that link bays with the Gulf of Mexico. Shrimp this large are less effective when fishing the bays, particularly around reefs, grassy points and on shallow sand flats. Larger shrimp are okay if you're drift fishing in the middle of a bay, fishing under the birds or working slicks.

Most often, it's best to hook a live shrimp just beneath the spike atop its head. Hooked in this fashion, the bait can swim about naturally. However, when the shells of the crustaceans are soft, it's generally better to hook them through the body, near the tail. (photo by A.C. Becker, Jr.)

It has been my experience that live shrimp about four inches long are the best for all-around trout fishing. Even when spiked to a No. 4 or No. 6 treble hook, shrimp this size are strong enough to move about in a frisky manner. They are also large enough so you can put them on the hook by spearing a tine under the spike or horn on top of the shrimp's head. A shrimp hooked in this fashion is able to swim about naturally. Whether you hook the shrimp under the horn or through the next-to-last section of the body from the tail depends upon the size of the shrimp and its stage of life. Very small shrimp are difficult to hook under the spike. There also are times when shrimp have very soft shells, and when you get them like that, the only way to put them on a hook is to run a tine through the body.

It pays to experiment when fishing live shrimp for trout. I have fished shrimp with the hook speared under the horn atop its head, and there have been times when switching to hooking through the body stirred the fish into action. Some of the old salts claim a shrimp hooked through the body swims in a crippled fashion. They base their contention on the adage that a crippled bait will attract a fish quicker than a healthy one. I used to fish with a guide who, just before putting the shrimp on the hook, would squeeze the head just enough to crack the shell. He claimed it caused the shrimp to "ooze juice and act crippled."

Speckled trout have large mouths, and when they strike they usually grab the whole bait. But this doesn't mean they wolf it down instantly. I observed trout taking live shrimp in a holding tank in a National Marine Fisheries Service study on feeding. The specks usually grabbed a shrimp, held it a second or two and then ingested it. I found it particularly interesting that over half the time, the trout grabbed the shrimp from the side rather than head-first. That's a knock in the head to the old rumor that a fish always swallows its victims head-first.

There are times when the fish nibble and peck instead striking hard. This usually occurs several times each year when the fish have what old-timers call "sore mouths." This is when the two canine teeth become very loose before, apparently, the specks shed these teeth. I have caught them with two long teeth, one long and one short, and even big specks with two very small canine teeth. I have caught trout when their teeth were so loose you could pull them out with your fingers.

When you run into this situation, hook live shrimp through the second body section from the tail, rather than under the spike atop the head. ''Sore-mouth'' specks nibble at the underside and soft parts of the shrimp. Sometimes they are like piggies and pinfish, in that they just nibble off the shrimp's legs. If you examine the shrimp very closely, however, you can tell whether it's the trout or piggies that have been nibbling. Unlike piggies, trout leave puncture marks and clean bites on the bait.

Specks will also nibble at the bait in the dead of winter when the fish are sluggish because of the cold. This is a time when the fishermen ought to use small shrimp, preferably ones with soft shells. It also helps in winter fishing to hook the shrimp near the tail, but through the lower part of the body.

MULLET AND MINNOWS

Other effective natural baits are small mullet and mud minnows. Two- to three-inch mullet and mud minnows are the best size for the general run of speckled trout. These baits can be hooked through the tail, through both lips or through the body just behind the dorsal fin. Whatever method you use, just be careful not to drive the hook into the backbone, or you will kill the bait. Mullet and mud fish stay alive longest when hooked through the tail. The frantic action of a tail-hooked mullet or minnow will galvanize trout into action if the fish are nearby. The action of a bait so hooked is similar to that of a crippled minnow.

Mullet and mud minnows are most effective in spring and summer fishing, especially when fishing jetty waters. They make poor bait in the winter when they may be stunned by the cold and be as sluggish as the trout. Other than appealing to large trout, the advantage of using mullet and mud fish is that neither is likely to be bothered by piggies and catfish. They will, however, become targets of blue crabs if the baits are fished on the bottom.

More anglers would use these baits if they were not so costly and difficult to obtain. You do not go fishing for specks with just a dozen pieces of natural bait. The number will be more like 60 to 100, and even this is a small number if the fishing trip is going to last more than three or four hours. At the time of this writing, most Gulf coast bait camps handling live mullet and mud fish were getting $2 to $2.50 a dozen. Enough to cover a day's fishing could run $20 to $25.

Ah, but you figure you're smart, so you buy a $30 cast net and decide to get your own bait. But don't forget you'll spend 45 minutes to an hour just getting the bait. Most fishermen consider it easier to buy live shrimp, which usually sell for $8 to $12 a quart along the Gulf coast.

DEAD BAIT

There are times when live bait is unobtainable at any price. The choice then is to use dead bait or artificial lures. Let's consider dead bait first, because a lot of anglers do not like to use lures. Their dislike generally stems from the fact that they don't know how to fish lures. It requires patience, experience and confidence to master the art of fishing with artificial lures. (See Chapter 4 for more details about fishing with artificial lures.)

When fishing dead bait, the first choice should be fresh shrimp. Any shrimp that shows signs of decay or has a foul odor should be discarded. The speckled trout is a picky eater that won't feed on stale bait or trash.

If they are small ones, hook the entire shrimp through the body and use it under a float. Jiggle the rod tip and pop the cork to put some kind of action into the bait. Dead shrimp can be fished on the bottom in the winter. Work it slowly the way one fishes the plastic worm in freshwater fishing for largemouth bass. Avoid using dead shrimp on the bottom in warm weather, because this is when the bait stealers are most active. They won't give trout a chance to get near the bait.

Try heading and peeling the shrimp before putting it on the hook. This will offer the fish a soft, easy-to-take bait, and it is a very effective way to fish the bottom in the winter. Trout are more likely to peck at dead bait than sock it hard as they do when striking live bait. The colder the water, the more sluggish the trout. Therefore, it helps to have some part of the dead bait on each tine of the treble hook.

When cut bait (mullet, piggies, etc.) is used, it should be scaled and boned. It, too, should completely cover the hook and again, it should be as fresh as possible.

BAIT FOR TROPHY FISH

There is a growing number of fishermen who set their sights on catching trophy-size speckled trout. Any speck that runs in excess of six pounds can be considered a trophy. There are not a lot of these big sows around, and fishing specifically for them can be mighty slow. You can improve your odds by using special

Though it usually involves a good bit of work, fishermen who want to save the expense of live mud minnows and mullet sometimes opt for the use of a cast net. (photo by Larry Bozka)

natural baits. Big specks have a weakness for small live fish ... croakers, piggies, and for some reason, small speckled trout.

When fishing around flooded grass flats during the peak spawns in spring and early fall, work these baits either suspended under a float or on the bottom with a slip sinker on a fish-finder rig. Small trout rarely bother these baits if the baits are six or seven inches long. Use either a slip-sinker or slip-float rig to fish these baits in deep water around jetties and in cuts and channels.

As mentioned earlier, I again emphasize that trophy speckled trout are few and far between. If you fish exclusively for the big ones, you are going to have some long, long waits, and there will be some trips with absolutely no activity.

To relieve the monotony, you might try the system I use: I bait one rig for big specks, cast out, set the reel drag very light and stick the rod in a rod holder on my boat. Then I fish a second rig for the general run of the trout. Always keep the rig that's baited for the big specks within easy reach.

Whatever kind of bait you use, it should be fished at least 18 to 24 inches below either sinker or float. It is important for the bait to have swimming room, for as it swims about, it in effect becomes a kind of fish-finder.

Sometimes a modification is necessary, such as when the bait swims up to the surface where the gulls may get it before the fish do. You can keep the bait down with the fish by attaching a split-shot to the leader about eight to 10 inches above the bait. When fishing the larger baits for trophy trout, you may have to use several split-shots, or perhaps a small pinch-on or dog-ear sinker.

BAIT CONTAINERS

A container that will hold at least three gallons of water will serve to transport live bait, if you have the means to aerate the water and keep the temperature moderate. Never crowd bait; give it living room. A container with four to five gallons of well-aerated water will support a quart of live shrimp all day. The best aerators are those that hook to the engine battery in the boat. Inexpensive, battery-operated aerators will do the job if you have an adequate supply of class "D" batteries on hand.

Both metal and plastic bait containers are available, but since you fish in saltwater, it is better to use only plastic containers. They stay free of rust and corrosion, so they last much longer than their metal counterparts.

The bait container should be round or oval. Square or oblong containers, unless they are quite large, are a sure way to lose bait. Shrimp, mullet and minnows are always swimming. They can swim in a round or oval container without bruising themselves by bumping into sharp corners. Bruised bait dies quickly, and dead bait contaminates the water and causes and additional loss of bait ... and the domino principle is set in motion.

Add chunks of ice to keep down the temperature to minimize bait losses in warm weather. If ice is not available, refresh the water in the container by changing it with the water outside the boat. Carry along a separate floating bait container that can be put over the side when you anchor or drift fish, and then put some of your bait in that container to keep from overcrowding the livewell in the boat. Any bait that dies in either container should be removed. Toss it over the side to serve as chum.

Dip bait out with a net and not with your hand. You may have been running the outboard motor and have fuel residue on your hands. If it gets into the bait well, you'll lose bait. Even the acid in the sweat on your body is foreign to marine life. Experiments on this have proven that the acid in sweat will actually repel marine life. Introduce it into the bait well, and you only excite the bait into becoming frantic. Finally, don't play games with the bait, like stirring it around with the bait net, a stick or whatever. It only serves to bruise and kill the bait. **BB**

4.
ARTIFICIAL LURES FOR SPECKLED TROUT

Fishing with lures demands a much greater degree of expertise ... and work ... than fishing with natural baits. Above all, the angler should strive to ''establish a pattern,'' recalling and repeating a productive presentation or retrieve. This sort of approach leaves little time for day-dreaming. (photo by Larry Bozka)

Speckled trout respond readily to artificial lures, and there are a number of fishermen who would not fish for them any other way. But successful fishing with artificial lures is an art that is not acquired by accident. It is a technique that takes time, patience and practice; and until it is mastered, this kind of hardware fishing can be frightfully unproductive.

But it becomes exciting and rewarding after the technique is mastered. In fact, some call it an art form that gives the angler a feeling of significant accomplishment because he, through his manipulation of the rod and reel, fooled a fish with a foreign object.

Very few fishermen will deny that they endured periods of frustration while learning to fish with lures. Successful fishing is not a lazy person's sport. You have to work to catch fish, and you often have to work hard. If there is any lazy aspect to fishing, it is when using natural baits, especially live baits. You cast out the natural bait and trust that its (hopefully lively) action and scent will attract your game. Meanwhile, you can simply gaze at the sky and daydream. But cast out an artificial lure and allow it to rest motionless on the bottom, and Christmas may arrive twice over before you catch a fish.

Fishing with artificial lures is work ... hard work. It is a repetitious game of casting out and reeling the lure back in, and then doing it over and over and over again.

That's only the beginning. If you are to be successful with a lure, you must impart action into that hunk of metal or plastic. You must try to think like a fish and then present the lure in such a manner that it will excite the fish into doing something about that thing wiggling by.

You must experiment with techniques. One day the fish may hit only rapidly retrieved lures. The next day only a slow, erratic retrieve will produce results. The fish may take only lures worked near the surface at 8 a.m., and then snub everything except bottom-bumping lures a couple of hours later. One day they'll take only spoons; other days, the trout may hit any and all types of lures tossed at them. And the frustrating part is that you never really know what causes the changes.

The speckled trout lure fisherman can't allow his brain to rest for a moment. He must be alert at all times. When he gets a strike or catches a fish, he must recall exactly what he did on that

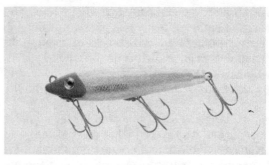

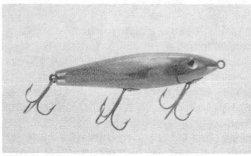

Note the difference in the positioning of the eyelets on these Mirrolure plugs. The lure with the eyelet in the nose is designed for shallow-water situations, whereas the bait with the eyelet above the nose runs deeper, and is better suited to use in the surf or deeper bay waters. (photos by Larry Bozka)

retrieve, and then duplicate it on succeeding casts. This is known as "establishing a pattern." Keep in mind that specks travel in schools and are often regimented in their reactions, except in the case of big, trophy specks, which are loners that have ways of their own. (More on the trophy specks will follow in a later chapter.)

Successful hardware fishing is both physical and mental work. But oh, how rewarding it is when you master the art. It is particularly rewarding in trout fishing because the specks respond to so many different types of lures. These include spoons, plugs and leadhead jigs, which are sometimes referred to as shrimp tails or bait tails. It is also interesting to note that some of the popular freshwater lures will consistently take trout. Specks can also be caught on fly tackle, although the number of fly fishermen on the Gulf coast is, at this time, rather small.

Regardless what type of lure you use, you must have confidence in it. Success in hardware fishing is largely psychological. If you have confidence a lure will catch fish, you will fish it in such a way that it will take fish.

I have a friend who fishes lures for speckled trout. Early in his fishing career, he made excellent catches on a spoon known as a "Dixie Bat." He fished that lure with supreme confidence, and he caught a lot of fish.

On one occasion when we went fishing, Tony picked up the wrong tackle box when he left home. We were 15 miles down the bay before he discovered there were no Dixie Bats in the box, but only bass gear.

I loaned him a Johnson Sprite spoon. I caught trout on the Sprite I was using, but Tony blanked with an identical Sprite simply because he fished it begrudgingly and without confidence. I know a lot of Tonys who feel lost if they are deprived of their favorite lures.

SPOONS

Speckled trout have been caught on spoons since the turn of the century, and for a great many years, the spoon was considered the only lure to use for serious speckled trout fishing.

Spoons are available in a number of finishes, but the ones most popular with trout fishermen are silver and gold. Any other colors used are usually the result of adding bucktails or plastic skirts to the spoons, whose popular colors include: red, white, yellow, green and black. Bucktails or plastic skirts that you add should be just long enough to cover the hook at the rear of the spoon.

A few fishermen decorate their spoons with various colors or shades by using fingernail and model airplane paints, or paints specifically designed for fishing lures. These paints dry in a matter of seconds, so some anglers carry several shades with them.

Silver spoons are popular year-round. The gold spoon is most popular for speck fishing in the spring. It would be nice to give a reason for this; the truth is, however, I simply don't know why.

Spoons are designed to wobble when they are retrieved. Generally speaking, small spoons wobble rapidly, while large ones have a wider swing and much slower wobble. The degree of wobble, of course, can be controlled by the way the fisherman uses his rod and reel. Dip the rod tip toward the water and then sweep it up or to one side rapidly, and your spoon will wobble fiercely as it darts through the water. Continue reeling as the rod tip is again pointed in the direction of the spoon.

Some anglers reel fast enough to keep the spoon in rapid motion. Others reel just fast enough to pick up line slack as the spoon flutters toward the bottom. This dart and flutter retrieve is popularly known as the "crippled minnow retrieve." It is a deadly way to fish spoons for trout in the spring and summer or when the water is generally warm. The spoon must be fished much slower and in a jigging manner in the winter, or when the water is very cold and the trout mill sluggishly in deep holes.

A special technique known as "skip-spooning" is an effective way to fish a spoon at night or in shallow water. When the cast is made, the rod tip is pointed at the spot where the spoon will strike the water. A split second before the spoon hits, raise the rod tip high over your head and reel rapidly. This will prevent the spoon from sinking, and it will cause the spoon to skitter across the surface. Small bait fish react this way when they are chased at night in shallow water. You have the additional advantage of attracting by sound in that the skittering spoon makes a "chattering swish" as it skates across the surface. It is a tremendous thrill when a big trout sucks that skittering spoon off the surface and takes off.

There is a lot of work in this kind of fishing, and it can be very tiring, but the rewards in big speckled trout make it worthwhile. It's not very effective during daylight hours, but the technique is a proven trout-taker at night.

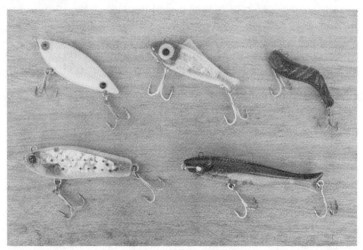

Given the right situation, a wide variety of plugs can account for speckled trout. The lure must be matched with the color and depth of the water, and success is dependent upon the willingness of the fisherman to experiment. No single lure retrieve will produce under all conditions.

Use spoons measuring two to three inches, not including the hook, in length. Keep in mind that the lure becomes about an inch longer when a bucktail or plastic skirt is added to hide the hook. Speckled trout will hit much larger spoons, but because of the fish's tender mouth, large spoons are easy to throw.

PLUGS

Spoons were the first lures used for speckled trout. Next came the plugs. The plugs, however, really didn't make much of an inroad into the picture until after World War II. Plugs were available prior to that, but almost all were specifically designed and promoted for freshwater fishing.

It was not until the late 1940s that lure manufacturers made big steps into the saltwater fishing scene. The move to saltwater got a big boost from a product developed during World War II; it was an easy-to-mold material called plastic that sped up production considerably.

The most popular plugs for trout fishing are slow sinkers and bottom-bumpers. Floating-diving plugs, strict surface plugs and jointed or "broken-back" floaters are, however, moving into the picture, particularly on Texas' Laguna Madre. These plugs can be quite effective for night fishing in shallow water, especially around flooded grass stands and on sand flats.

The slow sinkers and bottom-bumpers should be two to four inches long, not including the tail hook. A small bucktail can be added to cover the tail hook without radically changing the action of the lure. Plastic skirts are just as light, but they can "bunch up" and cause considerable drag that may spoil the action of the lure.

Plug colors can be any you find in the rainbow, and I know a few trout anglers who lean to some strange colors and combinations. But they've caught fish on the lures and have confidence in those colors, and confidence is the name of the game in lure fishing.

Most trout fishermen, however, lean to the following colors: red, white, blue, yellow and green. Fluorescent orange, yellow and lime-green are becoming increasingly popular. The most popular finishes include: perch, mullet, shad, threadfin and speckled trout.

Plugs are fished in much the same manner as spoons, although there is a lot more steady retrieving. Success with plugs depends upon experimenting until you start getting strikes and catching fish, and then sticking with that method. Bottom-bumping plugs are very effective for fishing in deep holes in the winter. Work the plug slowly in a hip-hop manner across the bottom. A yellow or white bucktail added to the plug increases its effectiveness in this kind of winter fishing.

LEADHEAD JIGS

After spoons and plugs come leadhead jigs. Actually, the leadhead jigs have been used for trout for many years, but they were never really popular until the soft plastic bait tails made their appearance.

These lures are nothing more than a ball or length of lead molded near the eye of a long shank hook. The eye, of course, is exposed so that the lure can be tied to the leader. The shank of the hook is then covered with the tail of a plastic shrimp, minnow, grub or worm. The most popular colors are red, strawberry, orange, lime, amber, white and root beer. The heads of the jigs are usually red, white, orange or black, and are complete with an eye painted on each side.

It has been my experience that the color of the head is unimportant. I have caught a great many speckled trout with leadheads that had all the paint worn off the heads. The wiggling portion of the lure, extending from where the hook exits to the tip of the tail, is what attracts the fish. These lures are usually sold in packages of one jig head with two or three soft plastic tails. If you run out of tails, simply cut one from a plastic worm used for freshwater largemouth bass fishing. Split the last inch or so of the tail so you can get an extra flutter on the retrieve.

I prefer to use tails that are either split or curved so they wiggle rapidly when retrieved. Most leadhead jigs on the market today are molded on single-tine hooks. Consequently, because of the single tine and the weight of the lure itself, trout can throw jigs much more easily than either spoons or plugs.

This doesn't, however, negate the effectiveness of jigs. It has been my experience, as well as that of many other jig users, that trout seem to respond more readily to jigs than to other kinds of hardware. It has to do with the softness of the lure.

Some fishermen object to jigs because they are armed with a single-tine hook. If you feel that way, you might look into a new patented leadhead jig, called the "Flex Jig," that permits use of double-tine and treble hooks. Another, called the "Cheater Jig,"

Leadhead jigs are arguably the most versatile of all artificial baits. They can be fished both under a float or on the bottom, and can account for a wide spectrum of fish species. Of these, the plastic shrimp tail (above left) is generally the most popular, followed closely by the plastic grub (above right).

sports a small treble hook at the end of its tail. This lure is especially effective on short-striking trout, as well as flounder.

The bait tail, which most saltwater fishermen call a shrimp tail, is a very compact lure that offers very little wind resistance when you cast it. This enables one to make extra long casts. This is very important in speckled trout fishing, especially when wading shallow flats or when fishing the birds. The leadhead jig is indeed an ideal lure to use with open-face spinning tackle. With just a little effort, a person can cast it the proverbial "country mile."

These lures sink very quickly. Hence, if you want to fish these jigs reasonably close to the surface, you must start your retrieve right after the lure strikes the water. Jigs are excellent for deep fishing, and are excellent trout lures fished right on the bottom in the winter. The retrieve can be either steady or jerky; or in very deep water, you can anchor your boat right over the hole and jig the leadhead up and down under the boat. Most of the strikes will come when the lure is falling after being jigged a few feet off the bottom.

The leadhead jig is a good choice for fishing under the birds, or bumping the bottom of bay sand flats or in the troughs along the beachfront.

The single-tine hook makes them ideal for fishing under the birds when the action may be of short duration. Hooked fish can be removed from the hook in a minimum of time so you can get back to the action. A major problem with using lures armed with treble hooks is that the school of fish may move out of your casting range in the time it takes to remove a fish from the hook.

COMBINATION LURES

There are times when trout fishermen resort to combination lure rigs. This is done most frequently when either drift fishing, fishing under the birds or fishing slicks. In the case of drift fishing, the theory is that the large lure up front attracts the fish, but the small lure trailed 12 to 18 inches behind is what excites the trout into striking.

The most common combination lure is one that is sold under the trade name of the ''Speck Rig.'' It is nothing more than a small wire spreader with a short length of leader attached to one side, and a longer leader to the other. A leadhead jig is attached to each leader. When retrieved rapidly, the lure resembles a pair of bait fish streaking through the water. This is a deadly rig for fishing under the birds, and it is a kind of rig that frequently rewards the fisherman with two trout on the same cast.

Other popular combination rigs include running a jig 12 to 18 inches behind a spoon or plug. This is a good combination to use when working the bottom in winter fishing.

Spoons, sinking plugs and leadhead jigs can be rigged to be fished under floats. They should be suspended 24 to 36 inches beneath the float. They are worked by simply popping the cork frequently to make the lures bounce up and down. In effect, the fisherman using this technique is appealing to two of the fish's senses. The popping of the cork appeals to the fish's sense of hearing or feeling. The bouncing of the lure attracts the fish's sight. And if you should happen to add some of the fish scents now on the market, you can also appeal to the fish's sense of smell.

Some fishermen have an aversion to using hardware because they consider lures expensive. That's not true if you analyze the situation.

For example, prices at the time of this writing for a quart of live shrimp are $8 to $12. Depending upon the size of the shrimp, the quart would contain from 30 to almost 100 baits. That same $8 to $12 would buy you a couple of plugs or spoons, plus three or four leadhead jigs.

The lures are expensive on a per-unit basis when compared with the shrimp, but the hardware becomes very inexpensive in the long run when you consider the fact that it can be used over and over again. You might use the two plugs or two spoons and jigs all summer before they are lost or taken away by a big fish, but live shrimp are usable only the day of purchase. **BB**

5.
WHERE TO FIND SPECKLED TROUT

Whenever there is a current, warm-weather fishermen will often find speckled trout in the vicinity of structures such as bay oil and gas platforms and pipe stands. These man-made structures offer shell pads at their bases that provide prime feeding territory for roving specks. (photo by Larry Bozka)

Cast a bait or lure into any Gulf or Atlantic coast salt water, bays as well as the surf and around jetties, and you might catch a speckled trout. That is how wide-ranging these fish are. You can replace that "might" with "almost certainly," if you know how to locate the fish.

Speckled trout are creatures of habit. If you catch them in a particular area during the first few weeks in May, you can wager you will get some there a year later, a year after that and so on, if the weather and water conditions are the same as in the year when the catch was made. It might be a week earlier or a week later if the weather and water conditions varied radically the previous month. I know a lot of skilled fishermen, saltwater as well as freshwater buffs, who base their fishing trips on their black books ... diaries of previous trips. Some keep their information on assignment calendars and refer to them year after year. I know one crusty old salt who has such calendars dating back 20 years.

But how about the men and women who have just started fishing? Or the folks who changed jobs and moved to the coast from inland areas. How can they locate speckled trout areas?

HYDROGRAPHIC CHARTS

Start with charts of the bays and areas you plan to fish. Hydrographic and navigational charts are excellent for this purpose. They accurately list obstructions, reefs, holes, cuts, channels, wrecks and types of bottoms and makeup of the immediate shoreline. All of these things add up to structure, and structure is just as important to speckled trout fishing as it is to largemouth bass angling. Next, correlate the structure with the season, time of day or night, and the habits and characteristics of speckled trout.

In the spring and throughout the summer, look for specks around the flats and grass stands in bays, around reefs and in the mouths of tidal bayous, and cuts on flood tides at night and early in the morning. When the sun begins to burn hot in late spring and temperatures continue to climb throughout the summer, turn your attention to deeper water ... holes, cuts, channels and middle bay waters.

Deep is the rule for winter fishing, too ... holes, boat basins, the mouths of rivers, and edges of ship channels are places to look for specks. In a severe winter, go to the deepest holes you can find, especially those that have some kind of structure to provide fish refuge from the current.

Seagulls diving and hitting the water are sure-fire indicators of feeding game fish. The fall months are generally the best for "fishing the birds," though spring commonly runs a close second for bird action. (photo by A.C. Becker, Jr.)

You can find all these things listed on hydrographic charts. All of the water depths listed on inshore charts will be in feet. Offshore charts list depths in fathoms.

TIDES AND CURRENTS

Pay very close attention to tides and currents. Both have great influence on the movement of speckled trout, or for that matter, on all forms of marine life. Specks move back and forth with tides, and they venture into surprisingly shallow water when high tides flood across sand flats and far back into grass stands. This is particularly true in the spring and fall, and at night. The fish retreat just as quickly to deeper water when tides fall. You are not going to find speckled trout marooned in isolated holes after the tide drops.

Correlate the tides with the water depths listed on hydrographic charts. You will find some excellent areas that can be fished only on flood tides. For example, if the chart listed the depth of the water over a sand flat at one foot, and the high tide for that day is 1.5 feet above mean low, then you will have 2.5 feet of water on that flat at high tide. That's plenty of water for wade fishing, and excellent for speckled trout fishing.

If you have sustained south or southeast winds along the western coast of the Gulf of Mexico, that tide could be pushed another half-foot to a foot higher. Southerly winds will do the same for the northern coast of the Gulf of Mexico.

Flood tides can push water far up into the marshes and lead to some fantastic trout fishing in the spring and fall.

On the other side of the coin, you can have winds that will prevent high tides from reaching their predicted levels. This will occur along the Texas coast if there are sustained westerly and northwesterly winds, along the middle Gulf coast states on northerly winds, and the eastern Gulf coast on easterly winds. This can become quite critical in the winter when blustery northers "blow the tides out of the bays," and tides run a couple of feet below their predicted stands. And this can happen over the entire northern Gulf coast.

Except in extremely cold weather, speckled trout are most active when there is moving water from a running current. Whenever there is a current, the trout tend to mill around structures like bay oil and gas platforms and pipe stands, along the sides and especially the points of reefs, around the land points that project out into bays, and along the stepoffs that border channels and cuts.

Moving water is an absolute must for trout fishing at the jetties. Whenever currents are lacking around jetties, bait-stealing marine life ventures out of the holes and crevices between the rocks. They come out in such masses that the trout never get much of a chance at the bait.

Biologists who have specialized in studying speckled trout report this species normally swims into the current, except when the current is very strong. The biologists also note that specks tend to work and feed into the wind and current, but they report that when the fish are spooked, they will turn and flee down-current and downwind. Fish are able to sense the direction of the wind by the movement of the waves and surface water.

LOOK FOR SEAGULLS

Use your eyes, particularly when you are fishing from a boat. Speckled trout are not going to jump out of the water for you to see them, but there are a lot of visual clues that point to the whereabouts of the fish.

Look for oily or glass-like slicks on the water; and pay attention to where the shrimp boats are working. Whenever you see shrimpers working inshore waters, you can wager there are schools of trout in the vicinity. Don't seek them in the wake of the shrimp boats, but work to nearby reefs and shallow sand flats where the shrimp boats can't go.

Seagulls are great for locating specks, especially when the trout are feeding and the fish are massed in schools. The gulls are most reliable when you find them milling over an area, screaming and dipping into the water to pick up bits of food. If they are picking up small shrimp, you can bet money there is a school of speckled trout working beneath the shrimp.

On rare occasions, the fish herding the shrimp may be gafftop-sail catfish, but when they are, the gafftops are big ones ... three pounds and up.

Even at rest on the water, seagulls are a sign of specks in the area. In this case, however, the fish are down deep and not herding shrimp to the surface.

Seagulls are the most reliable of the birds a fisherman may encounter working over salt water. White pelicans will mill around schools of trout, but only if there are a lot of easy-to-herd mullet in the immediate area.

Terns are the least reliable of all the sea birds where inshore waters are concerned. Terns are experts at finding refuse and ignoring game fish when working inshore waters. The terns, however, are very reliable for offshore fishing, and they will often be found working over schools of king and Spanish mackerel, dolphin, bluefish and jackfish.

Complete details on how to fish under and around birds are in the chapter entitled, ''Bay Fishing Techniques.''

SMELL AND SLICKS

Two less obvious ways to locate speckled trout are by the scent of the water or air, and by glistening slicks on the water. Locating the fish by slicks is relatively easy. The location-by-scent system is much tougher, and extra hard if you happen to be a smoker or partake of alcoholic spirits.

A school of specks can occasionally cause an area to have an odor a little like that of overripe watermelon. It is an odor somewhat like that found around a den of rattlesnakes, only the scent around the rattlers is much more like sour watermelon. If the scent comes from a stand of grass, an island, or a point of land jutting out into the water, I give the credit to rattlers and fish elsewhere. If a somewhat similar odor comes from an open water area, I immediately start hunting for speckled trout. I can sniff out specks if the school is fairly large and there is no wind to either dilute the scent or carry it away. I couldn't sniff out a pair or so of specks on a bet, but I know a few old salts who can.

Scent and slicks go hand-in-hand. When you pick up the scent, always start looking for shimmering, oily-like slicks on the water. These are easy to spot if the water is reasonably smooth, and if you can stand up in the boat to gain the advantage of height when looking at the water. When you locate a slick, ease around to the downwind side, and if your smeller isn't worn out, you should be able to detect the odor I described earlier in this chapter.

Remember, trout work up-current and into the wind, so the place to fish is on the up-current and into the wind side of the slick. The fish will be feeding up-current from the slick. If you fish the middle of a large slick, you may be casting to where the fish have been and not where they are going.

You can cast directly into slicks and catch trout if the water is shallow. If the water is deeper than five or six feet, then cast about five to 10 yards up-current of the slick. Remember that the deeper the water, the less likely that the trout will be directly under the slick.

Not all slicks pay off with fish. You have to work those that have just popped up on the surface. The most productive slicks are small ones, the size of a washtub. A slick this size is a new one, and it's a cinch a speckled trout is lurking nearby. When you see washtub-size slicks popping up all over an area, you can expect to get into some wild fishing ... you will be in the middle of a school of specks.

Old slicks spread out wide, and if there is a wind blowing, an old slick will take on a long, oblong shape. A single long slick isn't worth fishing because the fish have probably moved away some distance. If there are a number of these slicks, a fisherman should move up-current and up-wind to fish. Since in most cases specks feed into the current, they will be ahead of the slicks.

I have heard many stories as to what causes the odor and slicks. The most popular is that the trout cause both by overfeeding and regurgitating. I have caught specks and had them regurgitate in the boat, and the odor was as described.

I have caught a lot of speckled trout from slicks, but I do not recall catching many larger than about a pound-and-a-half in weight. I suspect the fish that make the slicks are masses of schoolies that compete fiercely for food. The competition for the food may reach a point where their stomachs just can't contain all that their eyes behold. Hence, they regurgitate. (This is also common with bluefish, especially when fishing offshore.) At any rate, speckled trout fishermen should never overlook slicks. The slicks pop up most frequently in the spring and early fall, the two times when trout are most actively working under birds in middle bay waters.

LOCATING BY SOUND

Sound plays a role in locating specks when fishing: (1) at night; (2) in flooded grass stands during the early daylight hours; and (3) in coves and sloughs in tide-swollen bayous and creeks. In each situation, the fishing is in shallow water, sometimes only a foot-and-a-half to two feet deep.

A big yellow-mouth sow speckled trout can make a lot of commotion and noise when it slashes into a school of bait in shallow water. Often the noise is caused by more than a single large trout. Sometimes a bunch of schoolies can make a lot of racket when the entire school charges through bait. I have seen schools make so much commotion that they actually spooked themselves back into deep water.

Speckled trout make a very distinct sound when they strike on or very near the surface. The sound is similar to that caused by a popping cork or Mansfield Mauler when an angler manipulates his rod. Judicious cork-popping around a flooded grass stand at night or early in the morning can frequently stir trout into action. "Judicious" cork-popping means doing it occasionally, not constantly or in a cadence. The point is to refrain from making the sound phony or mechanical-like.

TROUT UNDER LIGHTS

Many fishermen prefer to fish for speckled trout from piers, in bays as well as along the beachfront. Some are able to locate their fish by sight. If the water is clear and you are wearing glare-filtering, polarized glasses so you can look down and see deep into the water, it is not uncommon to spot schools of fish.

It is different at night when flood lights are beaming down on the water. These lights always lure small bait fish to the surface, and if you watch closely and look deeper beyond the milling bait fish, you often can see specks and other game fish. The problem here is that the light may attract so much bait that your shrimp or lure is "lost in the crowd" as far as the trout are concerned.

Believe me, it can be most frustrating. You see a lot of trout, but they only ignore your offerings.

The best technique to use in this situation is the one in which you make your bait or lure behave like a crippled minnow or shrimp. Jig the bait up and down. Lift it almost to the surface and then let it fall and flutter almost to the bottom. When reeling it back toward the surface, do so in a jerky fashion. Strikes usually come when the bait is fluttering back toward the bottom.

Beachfront waders can see schools of trout if the water is clear and wave conditions are just right. As long as the swells are not breaking waves, you can look into them and see the fish if the school is swimming near the surface. The challenge here is to get the bait into the water ahead of the fish. Some fishermen will cast right into the schools, the problem being that sometimes the splash of the lure or the float will spook the fish. This can happen when large lures are used or when live shrimp are used under big floats. With a little practice, you can learn to thumb the reel spool in a way so that the terminal rig will go into the water with a minimum of splash. This can be accomplished by casting low off the water, and then thumbing the spoon so that all forward motion of the terminal rig is almost stopped just as it enters the water.

SEASONS AND WEATHER

It is important finally to consider the time of the year ... whether the day is warm or cold, or whether it is a rainy period or a drought. Speckled trout are migratory only in the sense that they move back and forth from shallow to deep water according to variations of the temperature and the saline content of the water. Invariably, they are found in shallow bay waters when the temperatures are mild in the spring and again in early fall. They move to deeper waters along channels, into harbors and around jetties in hot weather.

Note in particular the term "along channels." The only time you find specks in the middle of a channel is when the channel is narrow. The Intracoastal Waterway that stretches from Florida to Brownsville on the southern tip of Texas, and the Galveston Ship Channel and Bolivar Roads between the North Jetty that stems off Bolivar Peninsula and the South Jetty that extends from the east end of Galveston Island, are good examples of this point.

Speckled trout are caught frequently from the middle of the Intracoastal Waterway, since it is only a few hundred feet wide.

The span between the North and South Jetties varies from a mile to a mile-and-a-half. Having fished these waters for more than half a century, I have caught a huge number of speckled trout along each side of this span. I have fished the middle of the channel where there was no boat traffic, but have rarely taken specks from the middle waters. Yet I have taken a number of bull redfish, large black drum and a variety of sharks from the middle of this same channel. Speckled trout certainly must cross the channel as they move from one jetty to the other, but apparently they don't linger very long out in the middle of the channel.

It is a waste of time to fish secluded coves and tidal bayous during or after very heavy rains or during periods of long droughts. Speckled trout migrate to waters where the saline content is relatively constant. Heavy rains, with their accompanying freshwater runoff, can cause a considerable drop in the salinity of bodies of saltwater not immediately connected with the Gulf of Mexico, where the saline content remains quite stable. Drought periods and high temperatures combine to deplete the oxygen in the water and run up the salinity. Again, the specks will move to more hospitable waters.

A good illustration of this is an upper-coast complex that Texas fishermen know well. It is a complex that includes Trinity Bay, then extends through lower Galveston Bay to the Galveston Ship Channel entrance and into Bolivar Roads. Trinity Bay is noted for exceptionally good speckled trout action under the

A good pair of binoculars can do much for the angler scanning the horizon for working seagulls. The trick is to look for movement rather than the birds themselves; they can be plenty tough to spot on hazy summer days. (Photo by Larry Bozka)

birds, drift fishing, and still fishing around the many gas wells, oil platforms, pipe stands and separators. Trinity Bay is bordered by land (mostly marshes) on three sides. Severe droughts and heavy rains that cause flooding on the bay's watershed will chase the specks out of Trinity. The fish move closer to the Gulf of Mexico and appear in large numbers around the North and South Jetties. They also fan out along the beachfront, where they offer fine fishing for waders and pier anglers. These fish return to Trinity Bay when that bay stabilizes its saline content.

You have a similar situation along the Louisiana coast, particularly around Calcasieu Lake, Vermillion Bay, Lake Pontchartrain above New Orleans, and the lacework of bayous on the Mississippi River Delta. It happens along the Mississippi coast in St. Louis Bay and around Gulfport and Biloxi. Alabama doesn't have much coastline on the Gulf of Mexico, and only Mobile Bay is affected by freshwater runoff. The Florida Panhandle and Florida Gulf coast have numerous bays in which speckled trout fishing is influenced by freshwater runoff.

FOLLOW THE CROWD

Two very obvious way to find where the specks are hitting are to check with the fishing camps and to follow the crowd. Bait camps are in business, and in order to operate successfully, the owners must get repeat business. You only get that kind of business by being honest with the customers.

If you are new to an area, follow the crowd. Look for anglers, particularly waders and those fishing from small boats. These are the people who are familiar with an area, and you can wager they will not be fishing for speckled trout in nonproductive areas. **BB**

6.
BAY FISHING TECHNIQUES

More and more, coastal anglers are turning to the use of electric trolling motors in order to silently approach slicks or working birds. Advances in technology have created a new breed of electric trolling motor designed specifically for saltwater use, and though they're not cheap, for the serious speckled trout fisherman they're well worth the investment. (photo by Larry Bozka)

T here are a number of techniques a person can use for fishing for speckled trout in bays. The weather and water conditions, time of year and phase of the tide will dictate the most appropriate to use.

The most popular and productive techniques include: (1) fishing the birds; (2) fishing slicks; (3) drift fishing middle bay waters; (4) wade fishing the flats; (5) fishing points and coves; (6) fishing the grass stands and small bayous; (7) fishing around oyster reefs; and (8) chumming for specks.

Each of these eight techniques can be done with both natural baits and artificial lures. When natural baits are used, they should be fished under floats to keep them out of the reach of blue crabs ... a problem in the warm-weather months.

FISHING THE BIRDS

Many anglers consider fishing the birds the most exciting technique. It involves locating the fish, stalking them to get within casting range, and then keeping alert to refrain from doing something to cause the trout to sound or leave the immediate area. A very challenging way to fish, it is ideal in the spring and early fall, when small shrimp are usually plentiful in the bays. It can also be done in the summer if the weather is mild and shrimp remain in the bays, but forget this technique if the summer is one continuous heat wave.

Fishing the birds places a premium on fast, seaworthy boats. Most of the fishing is out toward the middle of bays, where water can become rough in a hurry. A lot of fuel is necessary, and it is not uncommon to go through two or three six-gallon tanks in a day. Consequently, this kind of fishing can become expensive. You must eyeball the horizon all the time, scanning all points of the compass for gulls. Binoculars are a big help, enabling you to get a close look at the action of the birds so you can decide if a run to them is worthwhile.

Since this kind of fishing is in bays, you can forget about all sea birds except gulls. They are the most reliable, although there may be times when they put you over big gafftopsail catfish instead of speckled trout. Don't pay attention to gulls milling over ship channels proper, because they almost always will be feeding on marine life churned to the surface by the propellers of passing ships. The same thing can occur in the Intracoastal Waterway and similar canals with the passage of deep-draft tugboats.

Drift fishing is a good way to locate feeding specks. It's wise to carry along a spot marker so that the fisherman can mark the area in which the strike occurs, and repeat the drift over the same area. (photo by Larry Bozka)

Now to the specifics of fishing the birds: Obviously, you must find the birds first. The next task is to interpret their actions. If they are flying a straight course with a steady wing beat, or if they are flying several hundred feet above the water, you can forget about them. These are gulls bent on traveling. The gulls to keep tabs on are those meandering along about 15 or 20 feet above the water. These gulls are hunting, and they would not be that low or flying a weaving course if they did not see something in the water to suggest that shrimp might soon be herded to the surface. Get ready to start fishing if the gulls are helicoptering or milling in tight circles, screaming and dipping to the water to pick up food. These birds are over fish.

The cycle goes like this: First in the spring and then again in the early fall, small shrimp become plentiful in the bays. Schools of speckled trout, and occasionally big gafftopsail catfish, will work under the shrimp and herd them to the surface where they catch the attention of the gulls. When this occurs, specks often go on wild feeding frenzies, and they will strike just about anything that is tossed into the water. The fishing technique is to cast under the birds and around the edges of the area in which they are milling. If you can determine the direction in which the birds are working, ease ahead of them, stop the engine and let the school of fish and birds work to you.

There is no point in anchoring unless there is a complete absence of wind, but even then there will be slow movement as the shrimp are herded by the fish. If you are lucky enough to catch the wind and current just right, you may be able to drift along with the milling gulls and feeding fish. Otherwise, you will have to crank up the engine every time they are out of casting range. Then you will have to slowly swing wide around the area and maneuver your boat back into the path of the drift.

Success in this kind of fishing depends entirely on how you operate the engine. Speed is necessary to cover a lot of water in the search for birds, but with speed there is a lot of engine noise. Noise is much denser than the air above it, and water transmits sound approximately eight times faster than air. An outboard motor that may sound like a purr to your ears could be a roar to nearby fish.

So, while it is okay to run full speed toward working gulls, cut back the throttle when you are about a hundred yards away, and ease into casting range at slow speed. If your engine is a big one and the water is shallow (less than three or four feet), it will be necessary to stop the engine when you begin to fish. I have found you can get by with a small motor (20 hp or less) just barely ticking over if the water is about six to 10 feet deep.

Better yet, thanks to advances in technology and corrosion-resistance, an increasing number of coastal fishermen are turning to electric trolling motors for the ultimate silent approach. A quality electric motor is well worth the investment for the serious fisherman.

You can use either live shrimp or artificial lures for fishing the birds. Spoons and leadhead jig shrimp tails are my preferences. You usually catch a lot of small trout near the surface. They are the ones that sock the bait a couple of seconds after it hits the water. If the bait is allowed to sink three or four feet, you stand a better chance of tying into big specks. This is where artificial lures pay dividends, as the schoolie trout do not go for hardware as quickly as they do for live shrimp. Furthermore, the weight of lures causes them to sink faster than the lighter shrimp. This is one of those times when it helps to put split shot on the leader about eight to 10 inches above the shrimp. This will keep the shrimp away from the surface and out of reach of the feeding gulls.

Hovering and feeding gulls are the clue to immediate action, but they are not the only ones that can put you on fish. Keep an eye on gulls that keep getting up, flying a minute or so and then settling back, seeming to rest on the water. These gulls have found fish, but the fish are not cooperating in driving shrimp to the surface. The shrimp and fish are both deep, and usually the gulls are on the water almost immediately above them. Ease in close and work baits all around the birds.

Generally speaking, the more milling gulls you see, the bigger the school of fish. I have been right in the middle of a hundred or so working gulls and so close under them that I have had to sometimes dodge their ''calling cards.'' The number of gulls, however, is not as important as is the action of the birds. A single gull zigzagging and hovering can be the sign of a single big trout, and I mean big...six pounds and up.

FISHING SLICKS

Fishing slicks for speckled trout calls for a lot of boat running and looking around. And it helps all the while to sniff the air for any telltale whiffs of watermelon.

Slick fishing can be extremely productive in bays. Look for new slicks, small ones the size of a washtub or two. These are new slicks, and the fish that caused them are very nearby. After you locate a slick, maneuver the boat around so that it will drift toward the slick. It's important to be able to make long casts in this kind of fishing. You want to get the bait or lure into the slick while it is still a fresh one, but you don't want to run so close as to spook the fish.

Here again, electric trolling motors are the answer. A fisherman working an area that's holding fish can maintain his position and immediately react upon sighting a fresh slick. And you should constantly be on the lookout.

When you stop to fish a slick, don't devote all your attention to the slick you're fishing. Keep looking all around the boat for other slicks that may pop up. You need to exercise caution and make your moves with as little noise as possible.

Most slicks will be encountered in water up to about 10 feet deep. Small slicks are the most productive because they will be the new ones. Slicks that are hundreds of feet in diameter are old ones that may have been caused a half-hour earlier. Elongated slicks are old ones that have been stretched out by the wind, and are rarely productive.

Waders, too, can enjoy fishing slicks, although they won't see them from a distance as do the boaters. Waders have the advantage of being able to fish much more quietly than boaters, and when waders see slicks, they are usually within reasonably easy casting range.

DRIFT FISHING

Drift fishing is the third most popular way to find specks in bays. You simply allow the wind and/or current to carry the boat along. You cast and work the bait in the direction of the drift, for it is important that the first waters you fish are those that the boat has not passed through. Trout are easy to spook, and the shadow of a drifting boat can do just that. This is a real problem when drifting in water only three or four feet deep.

Drift fishing is a good way for one person to fish two rigs. Put a large bait on one and fish it on the bottom. Cast out opposite the direction of the drift and set the reel's drag light. Insert the rod in a holder on the boat and allow the bait to be dragged along the bottom as the boat drifts. If the drift is very slow the bait can be fished off the bottom by using a float. However, a fast drift under a float will cause the bait to plane to the surface. This kind of drift will occur when there is sufficient wind to blow the boat faster than the current. Even split shot on the leader won't help much. Whether the bait is dragged along the bottom or is carried under a float, this method of fishing is, in effect, a kind of trolling. It is an effective way to locate fish because a lot of water is covered.

Carry some spot markers in the boat. These are conspicuous float markers tied to one end of a line that has a weight at the other end. When you catch a fish, put a spot marker over the area, which will enable you to return to where the action occurred.

Drift fishing is most effective when you follow a pattern: Drift an area. Then run back to where you started the drift, move 10 to 20 yards to one side or the other and start a new drift. Without spot markers, you would never be able to find where you started the drift unless there were some prominent landmarks or channel markers nearby.

WADE FISHING

A lot of people, including many who own boats, wade fish for speckled trout. The general public seldom sees clusters of waders.

Wade fishing is without a doubt one of the most exciting ways to pursue speckled trout. A careful wader can get extremely close to feeding fish, provided he moves quietly and slowly. However, wade fishing requires the use of some specialized gear; for details see Chapter 13.

For one thing, most of the land that borders bays is privately owned, and if you do not have permission to cross the land, the only way to reach the wading flats is by boat.

Wading is really the only way to fish some waters. Specks are very easy to spook in shallow water, and when the boat is used, the bay bottom in shallow water can act like a sounding board in transmitting every beat of the engine. If one is to catch fish consistently in these waters, the fisherman has to get out of his boat when it comes time to fish. As far as this fishing is concerned, the boat is simply a means of transportation to and from the fishing grounds, and a resting place when one wants to take a break.

A careful wader can approach remarkably close to schools of speckled trout if he moves slowly and quietly.

The color of your clothes and the position of the sun in the sky must be taken into consideration when wade fishing. Remember, you are in the water with the fish, so don't wear clothes that are easy to see in the water or that will reflect light. This obviously rules out the sailor whites. Khaki pants or blue jeans are ideal. In cold weather, go with chest-high waders.

Shadows moving across the surface of the water will spook

fish in shallow ares, and wade fishing is certainly in relatively shallow water. Try to fish facing into the sun when it is low in the sky. This will put the shadows behind you and not out front where you are fishing. Remember, when the sun is low, your body will cast very long shadows.

Wade fishing is very popular in the shallow parts of expansive bays, where fishing may be productive in water just 18 to 24 inches deep. Sometimes the trout will be in such shallow water that they will cause swirls and Vs on the surface. Old salts call such a surface "nervous water." You just cannot fish success-fully from a boat when the water is that shallow.

FISHING COVES AND POINTS

Coves always support excellent trout fishing in the spring, for the simple reason that they are well populated with small shrimp and bait fish. Points that extend out into bays, or coves that indent the shoreline, tend to deflect currents. Speckled trout usually mill along the side of a point that is out of the current. They venture out to pick up food matter that is carried past the point by the wind or current. When fishing a point from a boat, anchor so you will be able to fish both sides of the point. Shallow waters in coves and around points are excellent places to wade fish.

A bank or stand of marsh grass a couple of feet high can protect a cove sufficiently so that it can be fished even in reasonably rough weather. In addition to boat and wade fishing, coves and points can be fished a third way...from the bank. Again, it is important to move slowly and quietly.

The tide phase is all important as far as points and coves are concerned. The fishing is always best on the incoming tide and high stand. If some sloughs empty into the coves, fish around the mouths from the high stand until about two hours after the tide begins to fall. The out-flow always carries a lot of marine matter that attracts fish.

FISHING GRASS STANDS

Grass stands are productive for trout in the spring, at night and early in the morning throughout the summer, and again in the fall, but only if the tide is rising or is already at the high stand. Grass stands support a tremendous amount of marine life, and when tides flood back into the marshes, speckled trout move to the edge of the grass to feed on marine life that swims or drifts out. Unlike redfish and sheepshead, specks don't actually move into the flooded grass, but only close to it when the tide floods. A couple of hours after the tide turns and begins to fall, specks will beat a retreat to much deeper water, and the action is all over until the next high tide inundates the area.

Most people fish grass stands from boats until the flats bordering the grass extend well out into the bay. Cast toward the grass so the bait will be within a few feet of the edge of the grass. If you have to wade and can't do it by moving out and casting back to it, step a few feet out from the grass and fish parallel to it. Once more, move slowly and quietly.

FISHING SMALL BAYOUS

The edges of small bayous can be fished by wading, but few bayous are so shallow that you can fish midstream waters without a boat. Speckled trout routinely swim far up bayous when tides reach flood stages. I have caught them five and six miles inland from the mouth of the bayou.

Bayous are loaded with structure, and these are the areas to fish. Work the edges of the bayou channel, the coves and openings to any sloughs that branch off from the bayou. Never ignore the small grass islands where bayous widen at turns. It is not uncommon for bayous to have small oyster reefs. These, too, are excellent areas to seek trout.

You can fish far back in a bayou when the tide is high, but reverse course when the tide starts to fall and go to the mouth of the bayou. Anchor the boat just outside the mouth, but close enough so you can cast back into the mouth proper. Fish the edges of the mouth as well as the channel.

FISHING OYSTER REEFS

Oyster reefs are alive with marine creatures, and on high tides they become rallying points for all kinds of game fish, speckled trout included. Some anglers dislike fishing around reefs because of the snags. Reefs provide fish protection as well as food. Look for trout on the sheltered side of reefs when the water is rough.

Fish the side of the reef closest to cuts and channels, and time your fishing to coincide with a rising tide and the high stand. With the proper footwear, you can wade fish oyster reefs. There is no problem with soft, mushy bottoms, although the footing can be a little trying if there are sizable clusters of oysters. Fish the ends of a reef when there is a current running, and be sure to work any cuts that may angle across a reef.

CHUMMING FOR SPECKS

It pays to chum for speckled trout. Use chum around the points and cuts in reefs, off fingers of land that project out into the bay, in channels between inlets, in bayous when water is moving and on sand flats. Chumming, however, is useless if there are no currents. You don't want the chum to sink to the bottom. Chum is only effective when it creates a slick behind the boat.

When trout intercept a slick, they usually follow it to its source. Chum is a good way to attract specks, but along with the trout come other species of fish, some good and some bad. A slick is good for attracting redfish, flounder and croakers, but it can be a headache when the visitors are bait-stealing piggies and catfish.

Years ago I used to chum with live shrimp. Every time I caught a trout, I would toss a few live shrimp overboard to "bait the water." Live shrimp are too expensive for this practice today, but shrimp left over from a previous fishing trip can be saved for chum on a future jaunt.

Remove the heads, because they rot quickly and make a stink that will attract catfish, not speckled trout. Dice the shrimp bodies with some finely chopped bait fish, like mullet or piggies. Pour the mixture in a half-gallon milk carton, add water to fill it within a half-inch of the top, and then put a length of cord in or insert a length of bent wire. Next, put the carton in the freezer and leave it there until the next fishing trip. The cord or wire is for a line to tie the chum block alongside the boat.

Blocks can also be put over the side in mesh bags. When you get ready to use a block, simply tear away the carton. Two or three blocks will do the job in winter fishing, whereas at least a half-dozen blocks will be needed for a morning in the summer. **BB**

7.
JETTY FISHING
TECHNIQUES

The author tends to a stringer of school trout caught by a group of "rock-hoppers." Walking the granite is often a slippery, strenuous proposition, and not one that should be undertaken by folks in poor physical condition. Fortunately, most jetties offer fishermen a short but accessible stretch of flat-topping. (photo by A.C. Becker, Jr.)

F ishing jetty waters pays off with a lot of large speckled trout, but this type of fishing is not within the
reach of every fisherman. To fully enjoy it, one must
have a boat, although on occasion, good trout action
can be enjoyed by "rock hoppers," anglers who walk out on the
rocks to fish. The problem here is that the rock-hoppers must be
as sure-footed as mountain goats. It's strictly for young people in
good physical condition.

Most jetties have a short stretch of flat-topping, or a stretch of
a few hundred yards where the boulders are placed in such a
manner that walking is relatively safe and easy, even where there
is a bit of surf running. Venture beyond that stretch and you have
a new ball game, a game in which the tops of rocks are as ragged
and jagged as a lava pit right after an earthquake.

Fishermen think of jetties only in terms of being good places
to fish, although the primary function of the structures is to
provide protection for the channel or pass that lies between two
parallel lines of rocks. A jetty is subjected to weather extremes,
the most violent being the storms and hurricanes that occasionally
batter the Gulf coast. Waves generated by hurricanes have awe-
some power, and if jetties were not constructed to withstand
nature's wrath, then granite boulders would be strewn in the
channels like confetti on the ballroom floor after the New Year's
Eve dance.

JETTY DESIGN

A properly constructed jetty is not just a pile of gigantic
boulders stacked up to form a granite wall. Rather, it is built like
a pyramid: where the width at the top of the structure might be 10
feet across, its base, 20 or 30 feet below the water, would be four
to five times as wide. Out at the seaward end where the currents
and waves are the most violent, the slope may fan out even more.
This is necessary to prevent erosion and collapse of the structure.

The huge boulders form the base for marine growth that is
attractive to a wide variety of marine life. Explore the cracks and
crevices when the wind is calm and the tide is low; the amount of
small sea life is astounding ... a virtual supermarket for game fish.
Wherever you find jetties in this world, you also find a rallying
point for many species of fish.

Gulf coast fishermen are fortunate in that they can fish the
jetties year-round. But as far as speckled trout fishing is con-

cerned, the best jetty action is during the warm-weather months, a period that extends from mid-spring to early fall. As in fishing for specks in other areas, the water around jetties must be reasonably clear and moving. If the tide is slack and the water is without movement or currents, jetty fishing for specks can be dismally slow.

WHERE TO FISH

The best areas to fish the jetties are close to the rocks, generally closer to the beach than the seaward end of the structure. The exception to fishing close to the rocks is when sand flats fan out along the beach end of a jetty. An exceptionally good area to fish is in the triangle a jetty forms with the beach. If the channel between the jetties is very wide, extensive sand flats can form. These channel flats provide good speck action for wade fishermen. The slopes to the channel are productive for small boat anglers.

Never neglect fishing in the vicinity of boat cuts or passes that may bisect a jetty. These are rarely more than 30 or 40 feet wide, and the water often boils through the openings during tide changes. The purpose is to allow small boats passage from one side of the jetty to the other. These passes eliminate having to go around the seaward end, where the water can often be dangerously rough.

As they're subjected to storms, and sometimes even hurricanes, jetties are built to last. Their bases are much wider than their surface area, which is why so much terminal tackle is lost by rock-hoppers. (photo by Larry Bozka)

Fish close to the rocks on the side to which the water is flowing. If the water is flowing from the Gulf side to the channel side, fish the channel side along the shoreward side of the cut. Fish the Gulf side and the length of the jetty toward the seaward end when the water is flowing from the channel to the Gulf side.

You have the option of fishing both the channel and the Gulf sides, if winds are light. Most old salts prefer to fish the channel side on an outgoing tide and the Gulf side when the tide is coming in, as long as the water is equally calm on both sides. The only times you have identical water conditions on both sides is when there is no wind, or when the wind is light and is blowing lengthwise up and down the jetty. Any wind that blows across a jetty is going to cause some chop and wave action that will wash through the rocks. The water that rushes over and through the structure will carry small marine life away from the rocks. This, in effect, "baits" the water on one side of the structure. Thus, the angler should fish along the side that is away from the wind. This will also be the side where the water is calmest.

LOCATING STRUCTURE

Boat fishermen can improve their success at jetties by using their depthfinders. This should be a basic for all jetty fishing, not just for speckled trout. When the water is calm, slowly travel the length of a jetty. Run about 20 or 30 feet out from the rocks and watch the depthfinder for structure ... holes, single large rocks, clusters of rocks and wrecks. Mark the locations by any odd configurations of the rocks atop the jetty, logs or timbers that may be wedged between the rocks, or do as some of the old salts do ... smash small jars of paint on the rocks. The paint seldom remains more than a few weeks to one month, but there have been times when Gulf coast jetties were polka-dotted with blotches of paint.

Occasionally, jetty fishermen take trout under floats, but this is usually when they are fishing close to the shore end of the structure, or right over rocks that are only four or five feet beneath the surface. Fishing near the bottom accounts for most of the specks taken from jetty waters. Any of three terminal rigs can be used: one is the terminal rig with a fixed sinker; a second is a slip-sinker rig; and the third is the slip-cork rig.

SINKER RIGS

Whichever type of sinker rig you plan to use, the sinker itself should be 18 to 24 inches above the bait. You want the bait to swim around and be moved about by the current. This motion helps to attract specks.

A fixed sinker rig is one where the weight is attached to the line in a fixed position, usually connecting the line and leader. Most trout fishermen who use this prefer a ringed sinker (small wire ring at each end) with a swivel attached for jetty waters. A swivel is a must if there is a lot of swirling current. Otherwise, you may have trouble with line twist. Other sinker choices for the fixed rig include dog-ear or clinch-on and rubber-core. All are streamlined. They can be cast with practically no wind resistance, and they have no sharp corners that will foul on the rocks.

The slip sinker is an oval- or egg-shaped weight with a hole through the middle. It is put on the line above a swivel that is 18 to 24 inches above the hook. The line will slip through the hole in the sinker, and this rig becomes a fish-finder in that the live bait and/or current can pull line through the sinker. You can cover a lot of bottom with this rig. It is also a terminal rig that is easy to cast.

SLIP-CORK RIG

A slip cork or slip float is one that has a hollow stick running through it. The line is threaded through the hole in the stick, and the float is rigged 18 to 24 inches above a fixed sinker. This is to prevent the cork from slipping all the way down to the baited hook. After the cast is made, the sinker will pull the bait to the bottom as the line slips through the hole in the stick. The amount

Close to the beach, wade fishermen often score by fishing right next to jetty rocks. The author advises fishing the channel side on an outgoing tide, and the Gulf side when the tide is coming in. (photo by Larry Bozka)

Boaters working baits near jetty rocks commonly boat nice catches of
speckled trout when the water is clear and the tide is moving. Extreme care
should be taken when anchoring; it takes only a moment for a drifting boat to
go up on the rocks. (photo by Larry Bozka)

of line that slides through will depend upon the depth of the water.

The purpose of this rig is to fish the line straight down so that
it will not chafe on barnacle-encrusted rocks. Some fishermen
prefer to keep the bait a foot or two off the bottom, so they tie a
small knot in the line above the float. When the knot hits the stick
in the float, the bait will stop sinking. You need to know the depth
of the water when using this rig. It is an excellent rig for covering
a lot of water, because the cork will be carried along by the
current. It is also the most practical rig to use when the bottom is
strewn with snags.

You can feel the fish strikes when fixed-sinker and slip-sinker
rigs are used. You feel strikes if you use the slip cork without a
knot in the line, although a hard strike will also cause the float to
bob. When a knot is used to control the depth at which the bait is
fished, a fish that strikes hard will pull the float under.

Always expect to hang a few snags when fishing around
jetties. It is frustrating to be catching trout and then hang a snag
that can be freed only by breaking the line or leader. This is an
occasion for using a leader that has a lower pound-test than the
fishing line. It is also the time to use a snap or snap swivel between
line and leader. Carry a half-dozen leaders complete with hooks,
so all you need do is snap on a new leader when you break one off

An electric trolling motor can be a big asset to the jetty fisherman casting from a boat. By slowly running near the rocks, boaters can work a lot of water in short order ... a plus for those who prefer lures to natural baits. (photo by Larry Bozka)

on a snag. Speckled trout fishing is like most other game fishing, in that the action can stop just as suddenly as it started. Thus, it behooves one to be prepared to replace terminal rigs quickly.

Another way to minimize snags is to use wire hooks that bend. A hard strain on the line will straighten out the hook so it will slip free from the snag. Then just reshape the hook with pliers and get back to fishing with a minimal loss of time. There is no point worrying that speckled trout will bend hooks. The hook will tear out of the fish's tender mouth before that happens.

ANCHORING AT JETTIES

Jetty rocks claim more than hooks and terminal rigs. They take anchors, too, but this is something that can be minimized by using special rock anchors.

But first, consider the best way to anchor a small boat near a jetty. Drop your boat anchor well away from the jetty, and in a place where you know there are no rocks or wrecks. Then use the engine to slowly back the boat toward the jetty. Ease close enough so you can throw a "rock anchor" into the rocks or atop the structure. Now with the engine still running in neutral, take in line on the bow anchor and at the same time, pay out line attached to the "rock anchor." Tie off both lines when the boat is positioned where you want to fish. This method of anchoring will prevent the boat from swinging back and forth. The main point is to have plenty of line out on the bow anchor so there will be sufficient scope to prevent the anchor from accidentally breaking free from the bottom. Remember, this is the anchor that is going to keep a sudden swell or wave from smashing the boat up on the rocks.

As for "rock anchors" I have two kinds, both homemade at cost of about two bucks apiece. One is a gallon paint can filled with cement. The other is made of several iron building rods bound together to form a shank with a bent-hook shape at the other end. The cement-filled can is tied to a line with a light cord that will break under a very stout jerk. If it wedges in the rocks, you can always get free by breaking the cord. Much stouter line is used on the building rod anchor. This kind of "rock anchor" will usually bend straight under a strong, steady pull. If necessary, you can jerk hard enough to break the cord attached to this anchor. You occasionally lose "rock anchors," but the financial loss is fractional when compared with losing a commercial anchor.

I have seen some expensive boats smashed and totaled out on jetty rocks because someone decided to pull up the anchor first, and then tried to start the boat engine. Outboard motors are dependable, but on occasion they have been known to be cranky at starting time. Always start the engine and warm it up before attempting to take in the anchor. Then slowly pay out line on the bow anchor and ease the boat back toward the jetty to free the "rock anchor." After it is freed, move ahead under engine power to pick up the bow anchor.

ROCK-HOPPING THE JETTIES

Finally, you can walk out on the jetties to fish for speckled trout. Jetty toppings near the shore are usually flat and even. Some are even flat-topped with cement for a few hundred yards. After that, the boulders come in many shapes and are set at many angles with all sizes of spaces between.

A fellow who is strong and in good health with a good sense of balance can rock-hop a considerable distance out when seas are calm and the rocks are dry. I have seen fellows rock-hop all the way to the Galveston South Jetty Lighthouse which is a little over two miles from the beach.

Ardent rock-hoppers match their tackle and gear to fit this kind of fishing. They carry landing nets with six- to eight-foot-long handles so they can reach out for their fish. Most use rods seven to eight feet long with fairly stout backbones. The length enables them to reach out to free terminal gear from snags and to keep fish from swimming into the crevices. The stout backbone and rod length will also enable them to land small fish derrick-style. **BB**

8.
BEACHFRONT FISHING TECHNIQUES

Along the Gulf Coast, wading the surf is a warm-weather pastime. Light winds and clear water are prerequisites to success, as is a moving tide. The same goes for the fisherman's ability to "read the water." (photo by Larry Bozka)

T here are three ways to fish for speckled trout along the beachfront: from a pier, by wading the surf, or fishing from a small boat. Each style requires special techniques.

The first encounter most fishermen have with speckled trout in the surf is through wade fishing. It is a different kind of wading than wade fishing a bay. For one thing, a beachfront wader must often contend with the force of breaking waves. For another, the sometimes incredible power of the moving tides can create dangerous undertows.

Yet, surf fishing is identical to wade fishing in that reasonably clear water and structure are needed. Clear water days along the beachfront are far fewer than in the bays. A 10- to 12-knot wind blowing in from the Gulf of Mexico is sufficient to cause waves to curl and break when the water shoals at a depth of about four feet. When that happens, the force of the breakers pounding down on the bottom will churn up a lot of sand, resulting in water that gets too sandy for decent speckled trout wade fishing.

Boat fishermen can get into trout action by fishing just outside the seaward line of breakers, if there are no more than four or five lines of breakers. (More about boat fishing the surf later in this chapter.)

WADING THE SURF

Wading the beachfront for specks is a warm-weather proposition, because the fish simply do not move into the shallow surf in the winter. Beachfront trout fishing months along most of the Gulf coast span May through September. Along the Texas coast, best weather is roughly from about the third week in April to the first week in October. The period along the southern section of the Texas coast usually ranges from early April to late October. Along the south Florida Gulf coast, the trout action generally extends from the beginning of April to the end of October.

In addition to the cold, the water along the Gulf coast is seldom clear during the cold-weather months. Weather fronts move from the northwest, and they all blow out into the Gulf of Mexico. Fall and especially winter northers pack a lot of wind, and the end result is very sandy water in all shallow areas.

Blue northers are particularly blustery, causing what old salts refer to as ''blowing out the tides.'' What happens is the wind has a capillary action on the water, causing it to blow back toward the

Gulf of Mexico. A blue norther coupled with a falling tide will cause tides to fall far below predicted heights, sometimes by as much as two to three feet. This is another factor that makes beachfront trout fishing practically non-existent in the winter.

The Gulf coast has some long stretches of beaches and a lot of surf in which to fish. You can catch speckled trout from just about any stretch of the beach front, but how well you score depends upon how close a particular beach is from a cut or pass that connects back bays with the Gulf of Mexico. Speckled trout are primarily bay fish, and if there is no connection with a nearby bay, you will not find a lot of trout in the surf even when water conditions are very good. This, in effect, means that every pass, cut or channel that ties bays with the Gulf of Mexico is fishing structure for the adjacent beach.

Wade fishing for trout is generally best in early-morning hours. The exception is when fishing from a boat or off a pier. As the day brightens, specks move out to deeper water and beyond the casting range of waders, where to get to them one must fish from a pier or a boat.

An important note to the surf wader: When the sand starts shifting, it's time to put on a life jacket.

Smart surf waders always wear a life jacket. Some complain that a jacket makes it difficult to maintain footing, as the fisherman is lifted with the waves. This, however, is no problem if the jacket is one of the "Mae West" type, inflated with carbon dioxide by the pull of a rip cord. The cartridges can be replaced as needed; each one provides a single inflation.

READING THE SURF

It is important to know the bottom of the area you fish. Be sure to fish around any rock beds or wrecks that may be in the area. There are also areas where one can wade out and fish alongside jetties. A stretch of beach where the bottom is covered with fine shells is much better for fishing than a muddy or clay-bottom beach.

Finding the right places to fish calls for one to be able to read the surf. This is nothing more than having the ability to tell from the color and action of the water what kind of bottom and structure there are in the immediate area.

The slope of the beach will determine how far a fisherman can wade out. Unless tides are unusually high, you can wade out far

This respectable four-pounder was taken near Vacek Bridge at San Luis Pass, a mile-wide cut located between Galveston and Freeport, Texas. The pass is a natural "highway" for big specks in that it serves to allow the continual flow of water between West Galveston Bay and the Gulf of Mexico. (photo by Larry Bozka)

enough to fish the second trough from the beach. A muscular fellow who can make extra long casts might be able to reach the bar immediately seaward of this trough. These bars run parallel to the beach, and are easy to locate when the water is rough enough to cause breaking waves. Waves begin to curl over when they reach a bar, and then tumble to become breakers that crash down into the trough immediately shoreward of that bar. This same wave will curl on the next shoreward bar and break again into the next shoreward trough. This will continue all the way up to the beach.

If there is a complete absence of breaking waves, you can still locate the troughs and bars by the color of the water. The water

Beachfront piers are available to everyone at a minimal cost, and allow boatless fishermen to reach beyond the boundaries of surf wading. Pier pilings provide fish-attracting structure that in turn draws feeding game fish. Coupled with clear water and floodlights, this combination makes for some fine night fishing action. (photo by Larry Bozka)

will appear light green over bars. The water in troughs and any cuts across bars will appear much darker green in color. In areas where the water is quite deep, the color of the water will be blue.

PASSES, CUTS, CHANNELS

Fish use passes and cuts that slice bars to move from one trough to another. These are easy to find. When there are breakers, look for areas where the line ends or shows less of a tendency to curl over. This is because the water is deeper in the cut than it is over the bar. These cuts are seldom sharp or pronounced, nor are they very deep. On a typical bar where the water may be four feet deep, the cut that slices across it may only be a foot deeper, and that cut through the bar may only be 10 to 40 feet wide. The cuts that slice the bars are caused by waves and currents. After lengthy periods of rough water, these cuts may be every hundred or so yards apart along a bar. In periods of very calm weather, bars may stretch a quarter of a mile before one finds any appreciable cut across it.

The really important cuts and channels to fish are those linking bays with the Gulf of Mexico. The waters on the Gulf side of major channels, passes or cuts pay off with a lot of speckled trout when the tide begins to fall, with the best action usually during the first hour or so after the high tide stand turns and begins to fall. This is a normal, local migration trout make in moving toward deep water when the tide falls. Most game fish found in bays follow a similar pattern on tide changes.

BAIT OPTIONS

Beachfront waders have three bait and terminal rig options. The most popular is fishing with live shrimp under a float. The next option is fishing with artificial lures, and the third is fishing live shrimp on the bottom.

A live shrimp fished on the bottom is listed last because any natural baits on the bottom are going to be attacked by all sorts of bait-stealers. There are times, however, when the specks are bellying on the sandy bottom, and the only way to work them is to put live shrimp down in their midst. Trout generally belly on the bottom when the water begins to warm.

Beachfront waders have caught speckled trout on artificial lures for decades, but down through the years there has been a marked change in the types of lures used. When I started fishing back in the mid-1930s, about the only artificials used along the beachfront were spoons. Once in a while you would see someone using a deep-running plug. Deep-running plugs, especially hard plastic ones shaped like shrimp, shad and piggies, made inroads in the early 1950s. This trend continued into the 1960s until one saw almost as many plugs used as spoons.

Then came the lead-head jigs. In the beginning, they were decorated with feathers or bucktails. Later, these gave way to jigs with the tail section of the soft plastic worm that proved to be such a deadly lure for largemouth bass in fresh water. In recent years, the worm tail has gotten very strong competition from shrimp tails, minnow tails and squid...hence, the term "bait tail." There must be 50 companies making variations of these lures today.

BEACHFRONT PIERS

When it comes to seeking speckled trout along the beachfront, more people fish from piers than any other way. When the trout are working the surf, it is not uncommon for a pier to attract upwards of a thousand fishermen in a 24-hour period. It is easy to understand why.

Piers give fishermen the advantage of fishing beyond the range of waders. Piers are ideal for night fishing, and when there is a rolling surf that keeps waders and boaters at home, you can still find a dry place on a pier where you may be able to tangle with some speckled trout.

Pier pilings provide structure that becomes covered with marine life, which lures bait fish into the immediate area. Speckled trout often mill around the pilings when the water is reasonably calm.

Finally, there is the advantage of having other fishermen trying their lures from the same pier. The addition of their baits helps to keep fish working the area.

Although the pier fisherman lacks the mobility of the wader and boat anglers who can move laterally up and down the beach, he has the distinct advantage of being able to fish shallow or deep water in all kinds of weather. He can also fish on a 24-hour basis. Neither waders nor boat fishermen can work the surf at night without considerable risk.

The period during which trout can be taken from beachfront piers is exactly the same as that for waders and boaters. On incoming and high tides, pier fishermen will obtain the best results fishing in the same troughs or on the same sand bars that produce for the wader. This holds for pre-dawn and early daylight hours.

When the day brightens and warms, the pier fisherman should move to deeper water. By mid-day or early afternoon, he may find he has to go to the T-head to find trout. This, of course, is the seaward end, where the water is deepest. The trout, however, are more likely to be on the shoreward side instead of the seaward side of the T-head.

NIGHT PIER FISHING

Speckled trout swim close to the beach when the sun sinks below the horizon and the darkness of night falls. If the water is clear and the tide is rising, specks frequently venture into surf just a few feet deep. When the tide recedes, the fish will move out deep. The pier fisherman seeking specks thus has a lot of fishable water, as the span extends from inside the T-head back shoreward to shallow water within 50 or so feet of the beach. He can cut down on the expanse of water he has to search by concentrating his efforts in areas where pier floodlights beam down on the water. The lights attract a lot of small bait fish, and along with the bait come the speckled trout.

Pier fishing can sorely test one's patience when it comes to landing fish. Small ones can be hoisted to the deck by reeling in as much line as possible, pointing the rod tip toward the fish and then swinging the fish aboard like a derrick. Just keep in mind that you may lose a speck or two because of their tender mouths.

Landing aids are necessary when you tangle with large trout. If the pier is low, a long-handled landing net will do the job. A better choice, especially from a high pier, is a drop net, a metal hoop 24 to 30 inches in diameter from which a mesh net is suspended. A bridle is attached to the metal rim and a long rope is tied to the bridle.

Lower the drop net into the water and let it sink a foot or two beneath the surface. Lead the trout over the net and then quickly pull up on the net. The trick lies in how deep the net is allowed to sink and when to start hauling it up. Never allow the net to sink to the bottom, for by the time you get it hauled back to near the surface, the fish will have moved. Start to pull the net up when the fish's head is just past the center of the net. Fish dive when they attempt to escape, and this dive will propel the fish right into the

When surf conditions allow, a boat gives the trout fisherman access to otherwise-inaccessible waters. It also affords mobility, allowing the angler to move up and down the beachfront while looking for signs of feeding specks. (photo by Larry Bozka)

net. But if the fish's head is beyond or outside of the rim of the net, the same dive will carry it free of the net.

SURF BOAT FISHING

The advantage of using a boat for beachfront trout fishing is that the craft gives you access to waters beyond the reach of wader. It also provides for moving frequently and quickly up and down the beachfront.

The baits and terminal rigs boaters use are the same as those for wade fishing: live shrimp under a float, artificial lures, or live shrimp on the bottom. in the case of boat fishing, however, you are going to be in deeper water and fishing at a time when the trout are relatively deep. Consequently, live shrimp worked on the bottom are far more productive than live shrimp fished under a float.

When it comes to artificial lures, stick with the bait tails when fishing very early in the morning, a time when trout are usually close to the beach.

There is a special spoon technique you can use if you can safely anchor the boat immediately seaward of the breaking waves. Use a silver or gold spoon with a large red, yellow, or white bucktail. Select the rod and reel that will enable you to get the most distance on casts.

Make the cast toward the beach, but don't allow the spoon to sink to the bottom where, coupled with the breaking waves, it might dig into the sand. Start the retrieve a second after the spoon hits the water, and then use a slow, steady retrieve.

This is one time when you need no rod manipulation to put action in the lure. The breaking waves rolling shoreward will put wild action in the spoon, and this appears to be an action that electrifies big trout. A three- or four-pound speckled trout hooked in rolling breakers will give you the fight of a fish twice that size. **BB**

9.
WINTER TROUT FISHING

Stocky specks like these can be taken during the winter months, but it requires a great deal more finesse than warm-weather fishing. Cold water makes the fish sluggish, and accordingly, the fisherman must slow the presentation of his lure or bait. The strike of a cold-water speck, even a big one, is often little more than a peck. (photo by A.C. Becker, Jr.)

Although speckled trout fishing can be enjoyed the year-round in Gulf coast waters, it can sometimes become a drag in the period that extends from late December through about mid-March. During these months, cold weather often makes trout very sluggish. Since the body temperature of a trout is that of the water in which it lives, the cold slows the metabolism of the fish. Trout in that state react feebly to fishermen's offerings, natural baits as well as artificial lures.

Sport fishing is supposed to be fun, and speckled trout fishing is fun ... for about nine months of the year. But with winter fishing comes more work than fun. First, there is the chore of locating the fish. With that done, you must work at enticing the fish to take baits. Through it all, you're suffering because of the cold.

Consequently, there are fewer trout fishermen out in the winter months than in the spring, summer and fall combined. Not that there isn't a certain amount of work involved in fishing regardless of the time of year; but in winter, the cold magnifies that work many times.

Nevertheless, if one has the fortitude to endure low temperatures and the patience to overcome the frustration of trying to get sluggish fish to bite, he can get into some reasonably exciting action during the frigid months. Additionally, if the winter is unusually mild you can enjoy a lot of good fishing with relatively little work. Gulf coast states have had such winters in the past, and will surely enjoy more of the same in the future.

EFFECTS OF NORTHERS

Throughout most of the South, winter weather fronts are called "northers." Winter fishing is affected as much by the wind that accompanies these fronts as by the cold. Weather fronts are frequent, and the more violent the norther, the poorer the fishing. Blustery northers that howl across the coast turn bays into masses of breaking waves, making the water much too rough for small boats. The capillary action caused by the strong northerly winds blows waters out of the bays, and the two- to three-foot tide drops leave wide expanses of glistening mud flats. The trout that might have been there during mild weather with a normal tide are now in deep holes and channels.

After the weather front blows itself out, there is the customary wait of a day or two for waters to clear and return to normal tide levels. A person can enjoy some reasonably good fishing if that period extends for four or five days. Often northers roar through one right after the other with no more than a day or two between, and when that happens you can go for weeks without any kind of fishing. The winters of 1977, 1978 and 1983 were like that, especially along the Texas coast, where temperatures dropped to record lows.

WHERE TO FISH

The first problem of winter fishing is to find fishable waters. Even between northers, fish-producing waters are limited and far less expansive than during the warm months of the year. Speckled trout go to deep water when northers blow out the tides and the temperature drops sharply, but the fish don't go to every hole or channel in an area.

They are seldom found in deep holes or channels where there are pronounced currents. It is supposed that the fish in their cold-

numbed state move sluggishly with the current until they are able to get behind structure. My experience in winter fishing has been to find the trout on the side of the hole that is protected from the current, behind structure that breaks currents, and in canals and boat basins that dead-end off thoroughfare channels. Currents are generally negligible in these offshoot bodies of water, where movement with the tides is simply up and down rather than in and out.

Speckled trout don't spend the entire winter in these deep holes. They move out to forage during the warming periods between weather fronts, and when the water is reasonably clear, you can get into some pretty good action in the bays. Skip fishing the flats or around grass stands unless they are very close to channels and large holes. The most productive waters during the warming periods are in the middle of bays, where the depth may be in excess of about six or seven feet. Techniques include anchoring to still fish around structure, especially shell reefs and

Winter fishing is as much affected by the wind as the temperature. Along the western Gulf Coast, "northers" create a capillary action which in effect blows the water out of the bays. The resulting two- to three-foot tide drops can leave wide expanses of mud and sand flats exposed. (photo by A.C. Becker, Jr.)

live oyster beds, or drift fishing. The fish will be deep, so work the bait on the bottom. Don't worry about those bait-stealing catfish and blue crabs, for they are seldom around in cold water. There is no point in looking for gulls in hopes of fishing under the birds, either, because shrimp aren't in shallow bay waters in the winter.

FISHING NATURAL BAITS

The number-two problem in winter fishing is bait. Live shrimp are always hard to obtain, and in severe winters there may be many weeks straight when all bait camps are without live shrimp. Additionally, some camp operators fail to plan ahead by stocking frozen shrimp in the fall, resulting in their going the entire winter without any natural-bait income. A bait shortage, live as well as dead bait, always keeps a lot of fishermen home during the winter, either because they don't know how to fish lures, or they dislike fishing with hardware. There were so few fishermen out during the winters of 1977, 1978 and 1983, especially along the upper Texas coast, that many fishing-oriented businesses simply closed shop for all of January and February.

Live shrimp are the best bait for winter trout fishing. They are usually available if the winter is mild, and if there are enough people going fishing to induce bait camp operators to go to the expense and trouble of trucking them in.

All winter fishing is on the bottom. Rig the terminal tackle with a fixed sinker about 18 to 24 inches above the bait. The sinker should be just heavy enough to enable you to make a fairly long cast. Remember, the fish will just peck at the bait, and too much weight will keep you from feeling the nibbles. There is no reason to use a slip-sinker because the shrimp may be too loggy to pull line through the sinker.

Get small live mullet or mudfish if live shrimp are not available. You may have to catch the bait yourself, as few camps stock this kind of bait in the winter. A cast net or a minnow trap can help you solve the problem. The mullet and mudfish should be hooked either through both lips or the tail, and they should be fished on the bottom and below a fixed sinker.

DEAD BAIT

If you have to use dead bait, select the freshest you can find. I always put a few packages of shrimp in the freezer just to be prepared for winter fishing. (Be sure to remove the heads before freezing shrimp to keep the bait from turning black.) Use No. 8 or No. 6 treble hooks, peel the shrimp and completely cover the hook with the bait. Fish this rig 18 to 24 inches below a fixed sinker.

Mullet, croakers and piggies make good cut bait. Scale these fish and carefully slice off strips that can be wrapped around the hook. Wrap them in such a way that each of the three tines will be covered. Some fishermen make split tails out of the strips and hang one on each tine.

Work all natural baits ... live or dead ... in the same manner. Make the cast; and as soon as the bait strikes the water, strip line off the reel until the bait hits the bottom. This slack will allow the bait to sink straight down to the bottom and not pendulum back toward the boat. You want to cover as much bottom as possible, and if you don't strip off the line to eliminate the pendulum, you will miss a lot of bottom. In winter fishing you must take the bait to the fish, because in their sluggish condition, they will not pursue a bait more than a few feet. The method of retrieve is to reel slowly and pause, reel slowly and pause until the bait is worked all the way back. Make each cast to a different spot so that a lot of bottom can be covered. Cast to the same spot only if you had a strike there and missed the fish.

FISHING ARTIFICIAL LURES

The artificial lures discussed in Chapter Three will do very well for winter fishing, although you may want to make some alterations to compensate for the fish pecking instead of hard-striking.

One alteration is to change your hooks to smaller sizes. Another is to hide the hooks in bucktails. This is especially effective on spoons and the tail hooks on plugs. Another variation is to remove the tail hook from a plug and attach a trailer lure to follow about a foot behind. The trailer can be a large fly, small spinner or jig, or a No. 8 treble hook hidden in a bucktail. The bucktail should be yellow or white. Some fishermen cover the trailed hook with fresh dead shrimp attached.

Some anglers make still another alteration on the trailer rig by streamlining a small piece of cork or foam plastic and putting it on the line about six inches ahead of the trailed lure. This will keep the trailed lure weaving in the water just a little off the bottom.

The most popular winter fishing trout lures are bottom-bumping plugs because of the two sets of hooks. The extra hook gives the fishermen better odds to hook fish that peck instead of strike. You get a lot of nibbles on the popular bait-tail jig, but because of the single-tine hook, you will miss a lot of hookups. A variation on the bait-tail jig is to use two small ones rigged on a wire spreader. These should be small enough for a fish to ingest when it is just nibbling. Used in pairs, these jigs have sufficient weight to make reasonably long casts. The same twin-jig rig (a commercial version is called a ''Speck Rig'') is often used when fishing under the birds in the spring and fall. When speckled trout are competing for food, this rig enables fishermen to catch two trout at the same time. Two fish at the same time, however, are a rarity in winter trout fishing.

LANDING THE FISH

The fact that fish just peck at the bait or lure means a lot of them will be lightly lip-hooked. This presents a landing problem. The fish may be loggy when they are hooked, but the sting of the hook and the pull of the line will light a fire in the fish. When the trout comes to life, you will have a whole new ball game. A lip-hooked speckled trout is a challenge to land, and one with a fire in its boiler calls for some deft handling on the part of the fisherman.

Few fish, even the small ones, will be hooked securely enough to be lifted into the boat or onto the pier. Therefore, a landing net is a must. Even wade fishermen should use landing nets in cold weather, as fish will be covered with a much heavier than usual coating of protective slime. If you think a speck is slippery to hold in the summer, just try grabbing one in winter ... with cold hands, no less.

EFFECTS OF FREEZES

The kind of fishing that prevails in an area during the winter will determine what kind of trout fishing one can expect the remainder of the year. Unusually cold and long winters can delay the start of spawning. This shortens the spawning period and results in a smaller population growth. Far more damaging are the periodic hard freezes that play havoc with trout in shallow saltwater bays. These freezes occur every 10 to 12 years, causing major losses of speckled trout.

Hard, sudden freezes that catch specks while they are still in shallow water can...and have...almost annihilated entire schools of the fish. Gulf coast states, and Texas in particular, have had freezes in which fish losses ran into the hundreds of thousands of trout. The fish are not killed outright; they are simply stunned by the sudden chilling of the water. The loss of fish occurs when the trout turn belly-up, float to the surface, and are blown in windrows into water too shallow for them to swim. There, they fall victims of gulls that peck out their eyes, gills and stomachs. These are these same gulls that lead fishermen to such exciting action in the spring and fall.

Another kind of trout loss occurs in the winter when netters are able to trap cold-stunned fish while they are still on the bottom in holes. During the winter of 1978, netters in Texas took approximately 200,000 cold-stunned speckled trout from holes in Trinity Bay. Trout fishing was poor throughout the entire Galveston Bay complex for the remainder of the year. The loss that winter was so great that in the next session of the state legislature, regulations were passed outlawing trawl nets in some bays during the winter months. More recently, a ban on all bay netting has been extended in Texas bay waters. Even so, there are outlaw netters still operating because so much money is involved.

The fish-kill during the freeze of the Christmas/New Year week of 1983-84 extended from Mobile Bay to nearly the southernmost tip of Texas. The loss in Texas waters alone was estimated at 15 million fish, including three-quarters-of-a-million speckled trout. That big freeze, which lasted 92 hours, caused an unusual speck run in the weeks following the thaw. Waters around jetties and along the beachfronts, in stretches of within a dozen or so miles of the jetties, paid off with large numbers of specks.

A winter trout run in the surf is extremely unusual. Seasoned fishermen and biologists believe the run was the result of fish that escaped the freeze by moving out into the Gulf of Mexico, where the water was much warmer than in the bays.

I have seen similar fish losses because of freezes occurring in Texas coastal waters in 1940, '41, '51, '61, '62 and '78. Prior to the '83-84 freeze-kill, the biggest loss was in 1951, after which the trout fishing along the Texas coast was poor for two years. **BB**

10.
TROPHY
SPECKLED
TROUT

Wall-hanger speckled trout like this Laguna Madre sow don't come by accident. Fish of this caliber are extremely easy to spook, especially in shallow water. (photo by Larry Bozka)

Most speckled trout fishermen go through three stages. The first is their start in saltwater fishing, when they are satisfied just to catch "some" speckled trout. That first stage quickly moves into the second, where the name of the game is to catch "a lot" of specks. That's the stage where you hear fishermen talking about limits. That desire to catch limits is long-lasting, usually for the remainder of one's fishing career. The third stage concerns catching big speckled trout. This is when you hear fishermen talk about "trophy fish" and "wall-hangers." This third stage, too, generally extends a lifetime.

Fishermen all along the Gulf coast have become more concerned with catching big trophy fish in recent years. The interest has been fueled by the many "big trout" contests that seem to spring up wherever saltwater fishermen gather. It used to be that the prizes in most fishing tournaments were fishing tackle and trophies. In recent years, however, awards have increased in value tremendously, offering loot like boats, motors and cash totaling thousands of dollars.

All of this raises a question as to how big a "big" speckled trout really is? At what point does the fish become a trophy? It used to be in the vicinity of six pounds; now it is closer to eight, although a fisherman need not feel that a six-pounder is unworthy of being made into a wall mount. I believe the minimum for a trophy has increased from six to eight pounds because so many more fish in excess of six pounds are now caught.

Let me quickly dispel the idea that speckled trout are suddenly growing larger; I believe it is more a case of so many more people fishing that the odds of catching specks in the eight-pound-and-over range are much better than they were years ago.

The biggest speckled trout I ever caught went a fraction over 10 pounds. But the biggest trout that meant the most to me personally was a six-pound, 12-ounce fish caught in 1945. That particular fish stands out because it won me a little silver medal in the annual Field and Stream magazine national contest.

Actually, catching a trophy speckled trout is more an ego trip than anything else. As far as I'm concerned, the table quality of speckled trout starts falling off after the fish exceeds about three pounds in weight. The heavier the fish is, the oilier and gamier the flavor of the meat. Or put another way, the steak of the yearling is tastier and more tender than that from a 20-year-old steer.

BEST TIME

If you are after trophy speckled trout, you had better plan ahead. Luck has a lot to do with every catch one makes, but don't leave absolutely everything to chance. Make some moves and preparations that will give you better odds.

Start with the time of year. Again, you might catch a trophy speckled trout on any of the 365 days in the year, but that's leaving too much to chance. You will be more likely to catch a big speck during certain periods, the best times during the spring and early fall spawns when the fish are heavy with roe.

Remember that almost every trophy speck is going to be a female. The males don't grow nearly as big, nor do they live as long as females. And this is in an area where I am at odds with the timing of some of the trout fishing contests. I have nothing against the contests as such; I just feel they should not be held at times when the females are getting ripe with eggs. Of course, the winning fish would not be quite so big ... a big seven- or eight-pound sow might weigh a pound or so less after she deposits her spawn.

The spawn that isn't deposited is a loss as far as propagation of the species and building the population is concerned. It's a point contest sponsors ought to consider. Properly promoted, it could do much to improve sponsor images, because there are a lot of negative feelings about contests within the non-fishing population. And that population far out-numbers the fishing fraternity.

Interestingly enough, the odds of catching trophy specks in the winter are reasonably good. Even though the fish may be sluggish from the cold, the big ones are more active feeders than the small ones when the water is cold. Furthermore, the trout are congregated more in schools. In the spring and summer, big specks tend to shy away from schools. They travel in pods of a half-dozen or so fish, and often the really big ones are loners.

Don't pass up fishing at night and under the lights. People who have homes and camps on canals catch a good many big trout by rigging overhead lights to beam down on the water. The lights attract a lot of bait, and with the bait come the game fish. The big specks usually swim around the fringe of the lighted area. If you're using artificial lures, try fishing large, deep-running plugs. If you elect to fish with bait, use a small piggy, croaker, mullet or large mud minnow fished under a float. Use the bait live and rig it to run three to four feet deep.

BEST AREAS

You could catch a trophy speckled trout just about any place you find salt water. But the fact that the water may be salty is no guarantee that big trout will be in the vicinity. Hence, if you are seeking big trout, you must go to areas where the lunkers are most likely to lurk.

Since I've already touched upon catching big trout in the winter, let's consider cold-water fishing first, (although it is not really the best time to try for biggies). The places to seek big trout in the winter are in deep holes where there is a minimum of currents. Boat basins and the dead ends of "clean" (pollution-free) ship channels are good places to fish.

During spring and early fall, work the fringes of saltgrass marshes early in the morning, at night and especially on flood tides. Spring and early fall coincide with speckled trout spawning. The roe is dropped in the vicinity of grass stands so that as soon as the eggs hatch, the young fish can move into the flooded grass for food and cover.

An interesting sidelight about speckled trout is that the fish are cannibalistic. After spawning, they frequently return to the area to feed on their young. In fact, before minimum size limits were placed on specks, I knew several old salts who used six- and seven-inch-long live specimens as bait for larger trout.

During the heat of summer, mid-bay structure such as oyster reefs, oil rigs and pipe stands, as well as wrecks and jetties bordering channels that link bays to the Gulf of Mexico, are ideal areas to seek large trout. The fish will be down deep.

TECHNIQUES OF THE PROS

The best way I know to get into large speckled trout is to fish with a guide. It is their business to follow the movements of fish, or they couldn't stay in business very long. Not only do they keep close tabs on where the trout are active, but they also have a few special little tricks and techniques they use to entice the big ones.

The main point to keep in mind about wall-hanger specks is the fish are extremely easy to spook. Obviously, the reason for their large size is their wariness and caution. If you fail to keep this point in mind, then you have a couple of strikes against you when it comes to catching trophy fish. This means a very cautious approach is necessary to the area you plan to fish.

Many fishermen seeking lunkers do so by wade fishing. They

Winter fishermen after big specks should try the ends of jetties and holes in deep channels. It's important to note, though, that these areas are most likely to hold fish when currents are at a minimum. Live bait fished on the bottom is the standard. (photo by Larry Bozka)

use a boat simply as a means of transportation to reach the fishing grounds, but as soon as they are there, they get out and wade. The reason is obvious: the wader can silently approach to the area he desires to fish. He moves with a minimum of noise, and he casts so his bait or lure strikes the water with as little commotion as possible. And remember, he is fishing in shallow water, and as he wades he moves away from the shadow of his boat. Shadows can spook fish quickly in shallow water.

Fishermen specifically seeking big specks pay close attention to what is occurring in the water, and are always aware of bait fish activity. Find an area where bait is active and you will find game fish. Follow that rule, and you'll catch a lot of fish.

As far as catching trophy fish is concerned, this rule holds just as true, but with the modification that since you are after large fish, the bait must also be large. The old salts claim that if the bait is only an inch or two long, most of the game fish in the area will likewise be small. So to find those trophy trout, look for areas where the active bait is reasonably large, five to seven inches in length.

After you locate active bait, the next question is: where should I cast the bait or lure?

First, determine the direction in which the school of bait is moving. If the current is light, the bait will be swimming into it. If the tide is falling, the bait schools will be moving toward deep water.

Some fishermen throw their bait or lure ahead of where the bait is moving. The experts, however, either throw right into the middle of the school or immediately behind it. The reason, they say, is that the game fish are following the bait fish and not swimming ahead of them. Those who favor casting behind the bait fish say the bait or lure is immediately placed with the game fish.

Those who favor casting right into the school of bait say the splash of the lure will startle the small fish, causing the school to explode in a spray and scurry fan-like in the general direction in which the school was moving. The fishermen employing this technique say the sudden commotion electrifies nearby big trout into feeding.

BAIT

What bait should you use? Young speckled trout feed almost

exclusively on shrimp. But as the fish grow older and larger, they turn more and more to fish as the mainstay in their diet. Hence, if you are after big trout, use a bait the biggies prefer. Small fish (piggies, croakers, mullet, mud minnows) are excellent for this purpose. Piggies, which are properly known as piggy perch, are hardy and when hooked through both lips or the tail, they flutter and dart about very much like the crippled minnow. This can produce electrifying results if big specks are in the immediate area. They will hit a darting piggy with a vengeance. You don't have to set the hook ... they will strike so hard they will hook themselves.

Let me digress for a few lines: I've caught large specks on small fish, live shrimp and lures. Those taken on small fish hit hard. I can't recall a single big speck (five pounds or over) hitting a shrimp hard. Instead of hitting hard, they just sort of sucked the shrimp in. But not all trophy specks are caught on fish or lures. I estimate about a fifth of the big ones I've taken were caught on shrimp. In fact, my first big one back in 1945 was taken on a piece of dead shrimp.

One of the best ways to stir big trout into action is to use a combination of a frisky live fish for bait and a specially rigged popping cork. The popping cork is rigged on a length of line about a foot long and between two swivels. The stick is removed from the float, and the cork is rigged by threading the line through the hole in the middle of the cork. If the stick in the cork is hollow, rig the line through the stick instead of removing the stick. Rigged in this manner, the float will slip freely between the swivels. It will stop against the top swivel when the float is at rest on the water. When the rod tip is brought up sharply, the float will slide down the line as far as the bottom swivel. Fishermen who use this kind of rig claim the resulting sound in the water is more of a "slurrrp" than a distinct "pop." Old salts say that small trout make a "pop" when they feed, while the large ones create a noise more like a sucking "slurrrp." There must be something in it, because these fellows catch a lot of wall-hanger specks.

In recent years, more and more people seeking big trout have turned to artificial lures, particularly large lures. They use jig shrimp tails that, overall (lead head plus tail), are five to six inches long. They have turned to large plugs, particularly the jointed or "broken-back" models. The shrimp tails with their single-tine hooks seem to be particularly effective when worked very close to grass stands on a flood tide and under poor light conditions.

There's also the combination of an artificial lure with a popping cork. The cork is used to attract the fish by the noise it makes. The popping cork used with a large shallow-running plug is effective for spurring big specks into action when fishing at night.

I can't help but take a conservationist's view of speckled trout in this chapter. It distresses me to see a person come in with a limit of specks five pounds or more, especially during the spawning season. I would like to see more of those big ones released so they can spawn again. Keep one or two for trophies, but release the rest. Just about every marine biologist with whom I've talked has expressed concern about diminishing fish populations, but more on this in a later chapter. **BB**

11.
HOW SPECKS STRIKE AND FIGHT

The fellow in the bow of this scooter is taking a chance by attempting to land his fish ''derrick-style,'' without the use of a landing net. It was a small speck, and he got away with it. Had the fish been a trophy, such a forceful technique would surely have caused the hook to tear free from the fish's thin mouth. (photo by Larry Bozka)

When a fisherman feels a fish pick up the bait, he must strike back hard to set the hook in the fish's mouth. This is the way it is with most species of fish, freshwater as well as saltwater. But fishermen who do this with speckled trout end up missing a lot of fish because they rip the hook right out of the fish's tender mouth.

Except in the winter when speckled trout may be sluggish because of the cold, there is really no need to manipulate the rod aggressively when you feel a fish working the bait. The hard sock used by largemouth bass fishermen to bed the hook when the black bass takes the bait is completely out of place in speckled trout fishing.

This is the reason some bass anglers are poor speckled trout fishermen. The same can be said for a lot of good trout anglers ... they just don't have the touch to be skilled bass fishermen. I am so used to handling speckled trout strikes that when I go for largemouth bass, I have to make a conscious effort when it comes to setting the hook.

Fishing only seems simple. It becomes quite complicated when you take into consideration the many species of fish, the characteristics that vary from species to species, and the various techniques fishermen must master in order to catch them. People become skilled fishermen only when they realize they must pay attention to what they are doing and work for the fish they catch.

SETTING THE HOOK

Speckled trout, except when numbed by the winter cold or during those periods when they have loose canine teeth, usually strike hard enough to hook themselves. Actually, all a person need do is to tighten up on the line to keep a strain on the fish. If he feels he should assist in setting the hook, then the strike with the rod should be with the wrist, or at most the forearm. The entire arm or two-handed socks are wrong. These jolting hits will sink the hook deeper if it is already in the fish's throat, but if the fish is only lip-hooked, such jarring strikes may tear the hook out of the flesh.

Every speckled trout fisherman wants to catch a trophy fish. It is a tremendous thrill when a six- or seven-pound sow speck takes the bait and sizzles line off the reel, but the bigger the fish, the easier it is for the creature to tear free from the hook. Yet I often see fishermen battling big specks with the gusto of a burly tackle sacking a quarterback, and then they wonder why they lose

Landing nets come in a wide range of prices, but it's wise to lay down the cash for a quality product. A good net will last for years if washed after each trip; better yet, it'll prevent the trout of a lifetime from gaining his freedom at the last moment. (photo by Larry Bozka)

so many fish. Muscles simply don't count when it comes to hooking specks.

HOW TO PLAY TROUT

Some people believe in "reeling the fish in quick before they get away," and in their haste to land the fish, they simply pull the hook out of the tender mouth. Remember, that tender mouth is the reason one of the fish's provincial names is "weakfish." Small trout can be horsed in and swung aboard derrick style, but be careful with trout in excess of about two pounds. You can make it a sort of judgment call in that if you see the fish is deep-hooked, you can take a chance on swinging it aboard.

It does not pay to attempt to horse in a big trout. "Once in a blue moon" you might be successful, but it is best to play the fish as long as it has fight in it. Bring a green fish (fish with fight in it) close to the boat or up near where you are wading, and the fish will still have the energy to turn into a wild acrobat. The fish may shake and flounce enough to tear out the hook, and there goes your big fish. I have had it happen to me, and it was not a pleasant experience.

Then there are the big trophy fish, yellow-mouth sows that run over six pounds. These fish deserve special attention. It could be a once-in-a-lifetime speckled trout, so play it to win. Don't gamble. Keep a strain on the fish and play it all the way up to the boat. Keep the drag set tight enough to maintain tension, but make sure it is loose enough so the fish can take line if it makes a sudden run. The reluctance of some people to let a fish strip line off a reel is what results in them losing fish. I went through that stage, and now as I look back, I could kick myself for letting some big trout escape. Trophy fish are not caught on every fishing trip. Look at it this way: seen in the light of fishing tournaments, the big fish you missed because of poor fishing techniques might have been big enough to place you in the money.

The proper way to use the drag is to loosen it a little when the fish is brought in close. Keep in mind that as the overall diameter of the coiled line on the spool increases, the amount of pull necessary to strip off line also increases. You can almost always expect a big trout to make a final attempt at escaping when it is brought close by. Always be prepared for that run to be sudden and quite strong.

LANDING SPECKS

Expert largemouth bass fishermen can reach over the side of the boat, grab the fish by the lower lip and lift it aboard. It's a hold that temporarily paralyzes the fish. Try this with a big speckled trout and you end up with a finger punctured by the fish's canine teeth. You'll also come away with a fistful of slime. Salmon fishermen often land their fish by grabbing it just ahead of the tail. Try this with a speckled trout, and the fish will squirt out of your hand, again rewarding you with a fistful of slime and a bunch of small scales for good measure. Instead, use a landing net to secure the fish. Buy one with a wide mouth, deep bag and a four- to five-foot-long handle.

There are correct and incorrect ways to use landing nets. Let's go over the correct ways first.

Put the landing net into the water before the fish is brought near the boat. Lead the fish over the net and then sweep the fish up. The sweep should be made from the head toward the tail of the fish. The move may startle the fish, but it will cause the fish to spurt forward and dive, and if the net is deeper in the water and a little ahead of the fish, the trout will dive right into it.

An alternate way to net, although not quite as sure, is to half-submerge the net and sweep it toward the fish head-first. This technique of netting works best if the net itself is of a color that blends with the water. A white net will make a trout, or any fish for that matter, make a sudden, sharp turn.

Some ways you should not use a landing net are, first, attempting to net the fish in tail-first. The combination of the hoop and net cause too much drag for you to move it fast enough through the water to catch up with a swimming fish, even if it is hooked. If the rim of the net happens to hit the tail of the fish, the trout will take off like a jet. Often this run is with such gusto that the hook will tear out of the fish's mouth. An even more certain way to lose the fish is to slap at it with the net as thought it was a tennis racket and the fish was a tennis ball.

LANDING NETS

Landing nets are available with white, blue, green or camouflage bags, and the mesh can be made of cotton line, monofilament or plastic-coated twine. I prefer green bags, with blue the second choice. Camouflage bags tend to look like seaweed and game fish simply do not take refuge in seaweed. The green and blue bags tend to blend with the water and are less easy for fish to see. A white bag will excite a fish and cause it to turn away.

Netting made of cotton line frequently fouls with the hooks, and you spend more time freeing hooks from the netting than you do removing hooks from fish. Monofilament, unless it is a bright fluorescent color, blends with the water, but the knots do not hold too well and sometimes the netting mesh has a tendency to skip. I prefer a bag made of plastic-coated twine. Hooks rarely foul in this kind of netting and the bag will not rot because of fish slime.

Purchase a net that will float. If the handle is aluminum or plastic tubing, remove the end cap and stuff the inside with bits of foam plastic or cork as a guarantee that it will float even if the tube springs a leak.

Landing nets come in a wide range of prices. A good one may cost three or four times as much as a "Saturday afternoon special," but in the long run, there is no question about it being the best buy. A good net will last for years if you simply wash it off after every fishing trip. If you don't, any salt that collects on the device will cause metal parts to corrode. Buy a good net and take care of it. Remember, it could mean the difference between a trophy fish hanging on the wall, or just talk about the "big one that got away.''

A personal experience will illustrate the point. As mentioned earlier, I caught a speckled trout in 1945 that won me a place in the Field and Stream fishing contest. The fish weighed six pounds, 12 ounces. Approximately a year later, I hooked a speck that "appeared" to be almost twice that size. But I lost that fish because the bag of my landing net was so old that it ripped under the weight of the fish. The fish dropped through the net, and the fishing line (silk that was about a year old) broke, and all I had left was the story of the big one that got away. I have only myself to blame, because I bought a very cheap landing net and had old line on my reel. Since that time I have caught several 10-pound speckled trout, but none looked as big as the one I let get away.

Use a short-handled landing net for wade fishing, or simply work the fish in close and then trap it against your thigh or waist. Remember, always approach the fish from behind. This is most easily done by leading the trout around you in a tight circle. While leading the fish, grasp it across the top and just behind the head, and slip your thumb and index finger into the gill openings on each side of the fish. Do it like you mean it; a hesitant approach will more often than not cost you your catch. And always, place the fish on the stringer before removing the hook from its mouth.

Some wade fishermen secure their catch with fish-grippers. You slip the jaws of the grippers over the fish's body, squeeze the handle and the jaws bite vise-like onto the fish. Grippers will certainly secure fish, but I find fault with them in that they don't float, and you have to keep them tied to a line around your body or hanging from around your neck. Furthermore, often they are metal, and unless you clean and dry them after every trip, salt water will eat away at the metal like a hound dog tooths a bone.

A wade fisherman without means of securing a fish can always walk the fish to shore. I did that one time with an eight-pound trout in the Laguna Madre. I didn't have a landing net, so I walked the fish back to ankle-deep water. Then I tucked the rod under my arm and grabbed the fish with both hands. (That was before I learned how to lock my fingers in the gills by grabbing the fish just behind the head.)

SPECIAL HANDLING

At this writing, there are no maximum size limits on speckled trout along the Gulf coast. There are, however, minimum sizes,

Speckled trout are delicate creatures, and if they are to be released they must be handled quickly and with care. The proper way to grasp the fish is just behind the head and the gill plates, preferably with wet hands. Take care not to touch the gills, and squeeze the fish no more than necessary. (photo by Larry Bozka)

and at this time they vary from state to state. It's the same with bag limits and possession limits. Hence, a fisherman must be aware of regulations covering the waters in which he fishes.

If a speckled trout is to be released to grow and fight another day, or even if you want it in perfect shape so it can be mounted, then the fish will require special handling.

When releasing undersized specks, try to use a minimum of hand contact with the fish's body. Care must be exercised to keep from wiping off the protective slime, as removal of the slime makes the fish susceptible to sores and diseases. Wet your hands first, and then squeeze the fish as little as possible when you are holding it. The ideal way is to keep the fish in the landing net when working the hook free. This way you can keep the fish from injuring itself by bouncing around on the pier decking or the floor of the boat. If the fish is only lip-hooked, there is no need to remove it from the water to release it. Simply grasp the shank of the hook firmly with pliers or a similar gripping device, and then shake the fish off the hook.

Never throw the fish back into the water. Make its return gentle to prevent shock. Release the fish upright into the water and facing into the current. If the fish appears to be fatigued, hold it gently and move it back and forth in the water in order to get a flow of water through its gills.

Special attention is necessary if you plan to have the fish mounted. Use a net to secure the trout, and then handle it as little as possible so that fins will not be broken, canine teeth broken off or scales brushed off. Gently fold all the fins against the body, and place the fish in a heavy-duty plastic bag. Close the bag around the fish, taking care to keep the tail flat. Put the bagged fish on ice until you get it to the taxidermist. If there is going to be a lengthy delay, freeze the fish after removing any air in the bag. Then let the taxidermist thaw it out when he's ready to begin work.

Scales on speckled trout are quite fragile. In fact, I have often scaled the fish by using a garden hose and jetting the stream of water against the side of the fish, working from the tail to the head and against the lie of the scales. The jet of water will take off the scales and slime at the same time.

Fish often have distinctive or unusual markings that are likely to fade out when the creature dies. If the fish is to be mounted, be sure to take some close-up photographs, preferably in color. Film is cheap when it comes to recording a historic occasion, and a trophy-size fish is certainly such an occasion. Therefore, shoot the entire roll of film, taking care to photograph the fish from all angles and both sides. The photos can help the taxidermist prepare you a really classy mount. **BB**

12.
GULF TROUT
AND
SAND TROUT

The gulf trout, like the sand trout, is much more plentiful than its speckled cousin. Though smaller and less desirable as table fare, the two species nonetheless provide hours of fun to fishing families. During the winter months, when the fish are migrating to deeper water, offshore oil platforms and wrecks often hold large schools that will readily hit cut bait. (photo by A.C. Becker, Jr.)

Although this book is about speckled trout, it would not be complete without a chapter devoted to the speck's common cousins, the gulf trout (Cynoscion nothus) and the sand trout (C. arenarius). There are frequent occasions when all three of these trout can be caught on the same trip. There also are times when speckled trout are scarce, but gulf trout and/or sand trout are available in sufficient numbers to take up the slack.

Gulf trout and sand trout are generally much more plentiful and easier to catch than speckled trout. Unfortunately, they are smaller fish and not as choice as the speckled trout. Furthermore, there are some variations in the fishing methods as well as the baits and lures needed. If a person specifically seeks gulf and sand trout, he should learn which are the most productive waters and at what times during the year the fishing is best.

When I started fishing back in the 1930s, fishermen recognized only two trout in Texas waters. As far as fishermen were concerned, these were the speckled trout and the speck's less regal cousin, the sand trout. Marine biologists, however, were persistent enough to finally get Texas and Gulf coast fishermen to accept the fact that the so-called sand trout could be either of two species.

The common name "sand trout" stuck to one of the species, but the biologists' common name for the other species, "silver seatrout," did not. Instead, Gulf coast sport fishermen eventually adopted the name "gulf trout." Some say this name was adopted because so many of these fish are caught offshore in the Gulf of Mexico. Others claim the partyboat operators are responsible for the name, in that "gulf trout" sounds more sophisticated than "sand trout." I can't see any point in fighting city hall unless it concerns tax matters, so throughout this chapter the two species will be referred to as every-day Gulf coast fishermen prefer ... gulf trout and sand trout.

PHYSICAL DESCRIPTIONS

The dark spots on its upper body, fins and tail immediately set the speckled trout apart from the gulf and sand trout. It is much more difficult, however, for the layman to distinguish between the gulf trout and sand trout.

The surest way to identify the two fish is to closely examine the fins. On the gulf trout, the spine and ray areas on the back connect, while on the sand trout they are separated. Note the anal fin on each of the fish. The gulf trout's anal fin has a count of 8 or 9 soft rays. That of the sand trout has 11 soft rays.

The gulf trout is the heavier of the two species. It has a tail that is a bit more rounded than square, as is the tail of the sand trout. It has larger and more pronounced scales, although the scales can still be described as delicate. The fish is dark greenish-blue on its back and bright silver on its sides and belly. The mouths of large females are yellowish-orange. The fish has a couple of canine teeth in the front of its top jaw and soft membrane around the mouth, as does the speckled trout. The average weight of a gulf trout is about a pound, although specimens exceeding two pounds are not uncommon. The Texas state record as of 1988 was six pounds, four ounces. The largest gulf trout are generally caught during the big run that occurs every fall, and most of the big ones are taken from offshore Gulf of Mexico waters.

Years ago, some ichthyologists considered the gulf trout to be a hybrid of the seatrout (C. regalis) and the sand seatrout (C. arenarius).

The sand trout is lighter in color than other members of the Cy-

The gulf trout is much more likely to attack artificial lures than the sand trout. Though most fishermen use cut bait or dead shrimp, some anglers score consistently with leadhead grubs or shrimptails. (photo by Larry Bozka)

noscion clan. The fish's back is dusky to straw-colored. It is most likely to be straw-colored when it is caught from the beach-front surf. The back of the fish is dusky when it is taken from deep water. The sand trout's sides and belly are silvery, but not the same bright silver displayed on the gulf trout. The sand trout is slender, has a squarish tail, and has the smallest scales of any member of the seatrout family. Its mouth is tender, and it has two canine teeth, relatively small, in the top of the front jaw. The average size is about three-fourths of a pound. Two pounds is considered very big. Because of the small size of the fish, the sand trout is often called a "cigar trout" or a "banana trout."

WATERS FREQUENTED

The gulf trout is quite common along the Gulf coast, and during the spring and summer, it is often caught along with the speckled trout. The gulf trout, however, migrates in the fall to the Gulf of Mexico where it winters in relatively deep water. These fish school around offshore structure such as oil platforms and wrecks. It is during this migration to the Gulf of Mexico in the fall, and the return migration back to the bays in the spring, when these fish move through cuts, passes and channels in large schools. Consequently, the fall and spring runs attract large numbers of fishermen, and during these runs it is not uncommon to catch a hundred or so gulf trout per boat. As large as these catches are, there is no talk about bag limits or size restrictions, so apparently gulf trout populations are high.

Of the three seatrout species found along the Gulf Coast, the sand trout is the most common along the beachfront, where these fish gather in large schools during the cold-weather months. These fish don't venture as far offshore as do the gulf trout. The sand trout is the "bread and butter" fish for beach-front fishing pier operators during the cold period that extends from late October into the following March. Catches of 30 to 40 fish per fisherman are common during this period.

METHODS OF FISHING

Both gulf trout and sand trout feed on shrimp and very small fish, and they will take dead bait just as readily as they do live shrimp. Hence, fishing for these species is much less expensive than speckled trout angling, because the high cost of live bait is eliminated. The gulf trout is much more likely to take artificial lures than the sand trout. When using artificials, use small silver spoons and small split-tail or flip-tail jigs.

Gulf trout are occasionally taken drift fishing, but it is rare to catch them under working flocks of gulls for the simple reason these fish seldom work near the surface. The best way to catch them is to find structure, anchor nearby and fish on the bottom. Good areas to fish for gulf trout are in boat basins that adjoin ship channels, holes close to the jetties, around wrecks and around offshore oil platforms out to about 10 to 15 miles in the Gulf of Mexico.

Rig a small treble hook 18 to 24 inches beneath a fixed sinker or a slip sinker. This is a good terminal rig to use if there is an appreciable current. Use fresh dead shrimp and wrap the bait on all three tines of the hook. Use whole shrimp if they are small; otherwise, break the shrimp into several pieces. Sometimes it helps to head the shrimp and peel off the shell. These fish are so plentiful during the fall and spring runs that some fishermen use terminal rigs with double drops so they can catch two fish at a time.

Sand trout are bottom feeders, and they are caught most consistently from piers and docks where a lot of fishermen are likely to congregate and bait the water. Most people fish for sand trout with double-drop terminal rigs. This is an easy-to-make rig with the sinker at the end of the leader and two hook stagings above it. Overall, the rig will measure 20 to 24 inches. Use peeled shrimp for bait, and break the bait into small pieces, placing a piece on each tine of the hook. When sand trout are caught back in the bays, they are often so small that anglers consider them a nuisance. They are much easier to catch in cold weather because at that time of year, there are very few piggies or other bait-stealers around to compete for the bait.

SETTING THE HOOK

Gulf trout usually strike hard enough to set the hook themselves, but the strike is not nearly so hard as that of a similar-size speckled trout. Sand trout, however, are more nibblers, and a person has to work at hooking them. Tease the fish by moving the bait in short jerks along the bottom. When you feel a pickup, use a wrist strike to set the hook. A harder strike will only rip the hook from the fish's tender mouth.

The gulf trout is the stronger fighter of the two, although

neither it nor the sand trout will test tackle, even on very light gear. These fish don't make runs like speckled trout. Their fight is a series of tugs and jerks, and they give up the fight much quicker than do specks. Neither of the fish are as wary as speckled trout, and you can make considerable noise and commotion without spooking them from the area. Although they have tender mouths, most can be hoisted derrick-style into the boat or onto the pier because they are small and not heavy enough to tear out the hook. Furthermore, they are so plentiful that using a net to land them is really a waste of time.

STORING THE CATCH

Gulf trout and sand trout die quickly after they are removed from the water, and their flesh spoils rapidly. They die quickly even when properly put on a stringer, and if they are left immersed in the water, the skin will soften and begin to shrivel. Overall, it is not an appetizing sight.

Store these fish by packing them on ice until you can clean them. Then put the fish in a plastic bag so the flesh does not come in direct contact with water. The flesh of speckled trout will also soften in water, but not as rapidly as that of gulf trout and sand trout.

Gulf trout and sand trout make good table fare, although the sand trout is so small that it is difficult to fillet without wasting a lot of meat. Because of the softness of the flesh, neither fish stores well in a frozen state. Freezing tends to break down the texture of the meat and you end up with something resembling mashed potatoes. Thus, these fish should not be kept frozen for more than a couple of weeks.

Both of these trout are really too small to cook any way other than to dip in a batter and fry golden-brown. One can fillet large gulf trout, but the meat of small ones is so soft that the meat will break into small bits when cooked. Then if you fry them just a little longer, the meat will break into a mass of crumbs. Treat these fish as you would panfish. Scale and clean, cut off the head and tails, roll the body in a batter and fry until golden brown. If the fish are average size, figure one gulf trout per person and two sand trout per person. **BB**

13.
SPECIAL GEAR

Of all the types of speckled trout fishing, none requires more specialized gear than wading. A wade fishing belt such as this one makes wading a joy, leaving the fisherman's hands free to handle both fishing tackle and fish. A fully rigged wading belt can hold a fillet knife, lure pouch, rod holder, quick-release stringer and a hook remover or pair of pliers. (photo by Larry Bozka)

Any person who intends to go into speckled trout fishing in a big way, and by that I mean fishing for them at least once a week, should think in terms of special gear and equipment other than the basic rod, reel, line, hooks, floats and sinkers. The mere mention of special equipment usually causes folks to shudder and visualize high prices. Fear not ... the "specials" covered in this chapter are not that costly, and are items that (given reasonable care) will last for many years.

In spite of the fact that speckled trout have tender mouths, they are sometimes troublesome to remove from the hook, especially when they take the hook deep in the throat. This becomes complicated when treble hooks are used, for there may be times when all three tines are sunk into the flesh. Digging out hooks with your fingers can be both time-consuming and wearing on the fingers. Consequently, you will need a device to make hook removal quick and easy.

HOOK REMOVERS

There are all kinds of hook removers on the market, and they range in price from less than a dollar to more than 10 dollars. Interestingly enough, most of the inexpensive devices are the most reliable. The problem with many of the costly devices is they have a lot of metal parts, including moving parts like springs and levers. That spells rust and corrosion when subjected to saltwater. Personally, the costly ones are much better-suited for freshwater fishing, where corrosion is less of a problem. Additionally, some of the deluxe, expensive devices are so loaded with extra gadgets that they are unwieldy to operate.

Some prying may be necessary to get the hook out of a fish's throat, and if the device has a tendency to bend or twist under a strain, it is not going to do you much good.

I carry several hook-removing devices in my boat. They include a plastic remover (very inexpensive but surprisingly efficient), long needle-nose pliers and three surgical clamps. The pliers serve a purpose other than removing hooks. They are perfect for re-shaping hooks after you have bent them out of shape wile prying them off a snag or from deep in a fish's throat. But pliers rust and corrode in a salty atmosphere, so I use mine as little as possible.

I prefer the surgical clamps. They are made of stainless steel

The fisherman who is out to catch his own live bait needs not only a cast net, but also an appropriate container for his catch. The ideal bait well has rounded sides, to prevent the fish or shrimp from injuring themselves, and provides adequate aeration. (photo by A.C. Becker, Jr.)

and are practically free from problems with rust. The big advantage is that after you clamp down on the hook, you can lock the jaws shut, and this will allow you a lot more freedom with your hands. Second, the clamps are long and slender and can be worked into tight places, and if the clamp jaws are curved, you can even work around corners. Clamps are available in many sizes and price ranges. Small ones at metal supply houses usually start at around $6 to $8. I have three clamps ... two are six inches long and one is 10 inches long. One of the six-inch models has curved jaws. I like the 10-inch clamps best, which have been used on everything from speckled trout to a water moccasin that decided to attack a bass plug.

I admit, it was not I who touched the snake; I stayed at the far end of the boat and let my fishing companion, a brave soul, grab the snake behind the head and dig the precious plug free with my trusty clamp. Personally, I would have cut the line and allowed the snake to take the plug as a souvenir.

But you never know how handy those clamps can be.

LURE CONTAINERS

Fishing with lures is no problem when you go in a boat or cast from a pier, because you can carry all the necessary gear in a tackle box. All that hardware, however, presents a problem for the wade fisherman.

You obviously can't carry everything, so the first problem is making the decision on which lures and how many of them to take. If you poke them in your pockets, you will have to keep them in plastic containers to keep from hooking yourself or your clothes. You have still another problem when you wade out deeper than your pockets. The plastic containers can fill with water and become a burden, or they can work free from your pocket and sink or drift away with the current. I have lost some favorite lures that way.

An ideal way to pack extra lures when wade fishing is to hook them on your hat, preferably a foam plastic helmet or a straw hat. I favor the foam helmet because the hooks penetrate the material more readily and they can be removed just as easily. A dozen or so lures add considerable weight to a hat, but if the helmet is made of foam, it is very light to start with. Furthermore, if the helmet is accidentally knocked into the water, it will float. A straw hat is a fine second choice, although hooks will sometimes foul in the straw and may require a little digging to free. Unless you rig your cap with a foam lure retainer, forget about lugging extra lures on your head if you insist on wearing a cloth or felt hat or cap. There are just too many snags.

Extra hooks, small sinkers, snaps and swivels fit neatly in the plastic containers in which 35-mm film cartridges are sold. The lids fit snug to keep out the moisture. Prescription drug containers serve equally well.

FISH STRINGERS

An ice chest is the way to keep your catch when fishing from a boat or off a pier, but there is no way to tow along one when wade fishing. That leaves the fish stringer or fish keeper net, or "Do-Net," as the alternatives.

The stringer needle can be either straight or curved, and it should be six to eight inches long so you will have some leverage. Most waders prefer the curved needle because it also serves as a hook to hang on your belt or on the suspenders of your waders. Stringers six to 10 feet long are ideal for wade fishing. You will need a stringer 12 to 15 feet long or of sufficient length to reach the water when fishing from a pier.

Always use a stringer with a float so the fish will be kept off the bottom and out of reach of blue crabs. In addition, it'll keep your catch away from you if you're wade fishing...an important factor when fishing shark-infested waters. For the same reason, the stringer should release quickly and easily.

The float should be big, at least five inches in diameter, to keep large trout from diving to the bottom. Another reason for a big float is that it is easy to find if you should miss looping the stringer on your belt or tying it around your waist.

Stringers are made of rope, nylon cord, woven strands of plastic, plastic-coated wire and metal link chain. The nylon cord, as far as I am concerned, is the only one suitable for trout fishing. It floats and it will not rot because of the slime that comes off the fish. Rope stringers soak up water and sink and are subject to rot because of fish slime. Woven plastic stringers are like saw blades, and if it runs back and forth through a fish's lips, the stringer will actually saw right through..and there goes your fish. The plastic-coated wire and chain link stringers will sink to the bottom and make your catch fair game for crabs.

The flesh of fish begins to spoil quickly when the fish dies, and a fish put improperly on the stringer will die within a very short time. The correct way to string the fish is to run the line through both lips. This will permit the fish to open and close its mouth to force water through its gills, which are to a fish what lungs are to a man. If you run the stringer through the mouth and out of the gills or vice-versa, you simply rupture the gills and cause the fish to die quickly. A fish that is put properly on a stringer, however, will remain alive for many hours.

Another fine item for wade fishing is the fish keeper net or

A foam plastic hat makes a great lure holder. A model like this will hold several dozen fishing lures. Although the lures add weight, if held on with a drawstring the hat will remain both stable and intact. (photo by Larry Bozka)

"Do-Net." This is a nylon net bag fitted to a foam plastic ring, the kind used for kids' floats for swimming pools. There is a drawstring at the neck of the net. You simply drop your fish into the bag, pull the drawstring tight and tie the device on a line attached to your belt or wader suspenders. Fish will stay alive all day in such a net.

WADING BELTS

Though some fishermen use nothing more than a leather belt to hold the aforementioned accessories, those who truly want to keep their hands free usually opt for a commercially produced wade fishing belt. The standard wading belt will hold a rod holder, fillet knife, lure pouch and box, pliers and/or hook disgorgers, as well as a quick-release stringer. Some will even carry cold drinks.

Several versions are available, but the main choice lies in the selection of the buckle. Some utilize metal or plastic buckles; others are simply attached via Velcro(R). Three Texas companies manufacture these belts: NuMark Manufacturing, Houston; Port O'Connor Outsiders, Port O'Connor; and Walk-N-Wade, also located in Houston.

ICE CHESTS

Coolers and ice chests come in many sizes and are made of various material ... molded plastic, foam plastic, metal or wood. If you do a lot of fishing, it is worth the extra money to buy a molded plastic chest. Get one that is sturdy enough so it can be used as an auxiliary seat. Metal coolers are heavy and will rust quickly when exposed to the salty atmosphere. Those made of wood absorb moisture and can become heavy, and unless braced properly they may warp out of shape. Foam coolers are very easy to break.

The ice chest is the only way to go if you fish from a boat. Don't skimp on size. The minimum size ought to be 48-quart capacity. A chest that size is big enough for mess of fish, some drinks, and ice or chemical coolants.

You can save yourself a lot of cleanup trouble if you keep a supply of plastic garbage bags in the boat. I slip my fish into such a bag before I put the fish in the cooler. This will protect everything in the cooler from slime, scales and blood. Use dish washing liquid and fresh water to clean the inside of the cooler. Rinse out the suds, then put in a gallon or so of fresh water with a little lemon juice added. Swirl it around a few times and all the fish odors will vanish. Dry the inside, prop the lid open and let it air out overnight. With just cursory care, a good cooler will last many years.

CHEMICAL COOLANTS

I frequently use chemical coolants instead of crushed or block ice in my cooler. For one thing the frozen chemical blocks thaw much more slowly than ice. When ice melts, you have a lot of water sloshing around in the bottom of the cooler. You don't have this problem with chemical blocks, which can be re-frozen and used time after time. Hose off the blocks after each trip and put them back in the freezer so they will be ready for the next trip. They are a little heavier than ice blocks of similar size, but they come in various sizes so you can pack them around the parts you want to keep cool.

If you elect to use ice instead of chemical coolants, be sure to keep draining the water from the cooler, and don't let any dead fish slip down into the water. Even though the water is cold, it will soften the meat. Fish can be stored without loss of flavor or texture on top of ice, packed in ice, but not immersed in water, even if the water is cold.

FISHING KNIVES

A pocket knife is not a fishing knife, although it will do in a pinch. There are fishing knives and there are so-called fishing knives. Some have so many "useful attachments" (manufacturer's claims) that they have become gadgets instead of knives. Forget the frills and simply purchase a good fillet knife.

All knives exposed to the salt atmosphere take a beating, so if you expect to get long service out of a knife, it should be washed and thoroughly dried after each fishing trip. Take another minute or two to give it a few licks on a whetstone so it will have a keen edge for the next fishing trip. Then place it in a dry place.

Blade length is matter of personal preference. I like a knife with a five- to six-inch blade that tapers to a sharp point. Fishing knives come with all kinds of handles, some functional and some just pretty. Purchase a knife with handles designed to keep it afloat in case it is dropped overboard. It is curious to note how often people describe losing a knife as "falling overboard." They never admit to dropping it.

FISH SCALERS

There are almost as many devices for scaling fish as there are hook removers. The slime that covers the fish is what makes scaling seem a chore. As I described in an earlier chapter, I have knocked off both slime and scales from average-size speckled trout with a garden hose by jetting a stream of water against the lie of the scales. This means working from the tail to the head of the fish. But don't do this indoors or within the city. Neighbors have been known to object to little rivers of water carrying fish slime and scales down the street.

You can use a tablespoon to scale most members of the Cynoscion family. Work from the tail to the head and cup your hand over the spoon to catch the scales as they come off. You can do the same thing with an oyster or clam shell.

Don't purchase a scaler with large, sharp teeth because a little too much force with such an instrument will score, cut or bruise the flesh. For example, a scaler suitable to work a heavy-scaled fish like a redfish or red snapper will be too coarse for speckled trout. By the same token, the perfect speckled trout scaler isn't going to dent a big redfish or snapper.

CLEANSING AGENTS

A bar of soap is a very useful item in a fishing boat, and there are times, in fact, when a bar of soap can directly influence your fishing success. You should wash your hands with soap, or a commercial odor-remover like Berkley "Erase," every time you change fuel tanks or fiddle with any part of the engine that may have oil or gas residue on it. That residue could get into your bait container and kill all your bait.

Keep an old toothbrush and a small tube of toothpaste in the tackle box. They are good for scrubbing mildew or tarnish off plugs and spoons. Use the brush and paste to scrub the outside of reels and rod reelseats.

STINGRAY LEGGINGS

The fishermen who swear most by these are those who have endured the agony of a stingray wound. Though shuffling the feet will most often move these swimming "land mines" out of the way, there are exceptions.

The only fool-proof means of protection exists in the form of stingray leggings. Constructed of layered ballistics cloth, the nylon leggings will stop a .38 bullet. They fit over the boot or shoe, and are held in place by Velcro(R) straps. They are also effective in protecting your legs while out of the water from everything from snakes to prickly pear thorns. In the water, the leggings provide a shield from unseen crab traps, rocks, and other sunken but hazardous debris.

These leggings, which will last a lifetime, are currently available from Paul Perrin of Walk-N-Wade, based in Houston.

TACKLE HANDLING TECHNIQUES

Finally, there are tackle handling techniques that can lessen fatigue that comes from long hours of fishing. The techniques have to do with the manner in which you hold your gear.

Tighten your fingers and hand into a ball. You cannot maintain this posture for any length of time without the forearm muscles beginning to ache. The normal posture of the hand and fingers is relaxed and slightly cupped. You can go around like this all day and never tax the forearm muscles.

The diameter of a rod handle is small, and wrapping one's hands and fingers tightly around it will tire the forearm muscles.

The author prepares to add another nice trout to his "Do-Net." The nylon net bag allows fish to remain alive for hours while the foam plastic ring keeps the catch off the bottom and away from crabs. Made in Houston, Texas, by NuMark Manufacturing, this product is especially useful when wade fishing. (photo by A.C. Becker, Jr.)

You find a parallel in people who "white-knuckle" (tightly grip) the steering wheel while driving. You have to hold the rod tightly when you cast, but you can lessen the strain on the muscles by "palming the reel" while you are waiting for a strike or working the bait or lure.

Instead of holding the rod handle, you hold the reel in the palm of your hand. You can hold it securely by slightly cupping the hands and fingers. Use the other hand to crank the reel handle. Note that the side of the reel, not the top or bottom, is palmed in the hand. Also note that neither hand is in direct contact with the reel handle, yet when the reel is "palmed," the rod handle runs parallel to and against the forearm. In effect, this makes the forearm a apart of the handle. This is a very comfortable way to fish light to medium tackle, and you can do it with baitcasting and spin-cast reels.

The open-face spinning reel hangs below the rod, and is less tiring than a rig that requires a grip on the handle or reel to keep the rig from flipping over. There is a comfortable way to hold spinning gear. Hold the rod so that the leg of the reel is between the index and fourth fingers of your hand. If the rod is a proper match with the reel, the entire rig will balance in your hand. Again, you can fish the rig with a loosely cupped hand instead of a death-grip around a relatively small-diameter handle. You can still grip the handle tightly and very quickly when you hook a fish. **BB**

14.
WHAT
THE FUTURE
HOLDS

If youngsters like this little tyke are to enjoy quality fishing in the future, fishermen have to remain conscious of the need for conservation. Recreational anglers have always stood in the forefront of conservation efforts, and that trend is not likely to change in coming years. (photo by Larry Bozka)

Although Gulf coast states have had game and fish departments for many decades, saltwater fisheries management is relatively new. Only in comparatively recent years have studies advanced enough for intelligent estimates to be made on fish populations and harvests, and as a result we are seeing more and more fish brought under varying degrees of protection. This protection has come in the form of size and/or bag limits, methods of harvest and regulations for the protection of nursery grounds. More and more fish are being classified as game fish. This is the first step toward taking a fish off the commercial market.

The sea, which was formerly thought to be inexhaustible as far as marine life was concerned, is now being assisted by legislation, laboratory breeding and spawning programs. Without these many forms of assistance, marine life would face extinction.

There are many threats to the existence and range of speckled trout in Gulf coast waters. There is greatly increased fishing pressure, sport as well as commercial. There are major changes in the breeding and nursery grounds because of environmental alterations. Some fish-taking methods are so efficient (from man's standpoint) that areas can be harvested almost clean of fish, food fish as well as rough fish. And finally there is pollution, a curse that has made some water almost barren of all forms of marine life.

What has happened, and is continuing to happen, cannot be glossed over in a single sentence. Elaboration is necessary on each of the points if the reader is to understand the impact of the whole picture, and then be able to look ahead to what the future may hold.

HOW IT USED TO BE

To understand where we are headed, it is necessary to look at what we have today in terms of what we had two, three, four or five decades ago as a basis for comparison.

When I started fishing in the 1930s, there was no such thing as fishing pressure. My father had a camp on Galveston Island, and at the time it was "down the island" on Sydnor's Bayou. It was six miles outside the city limits, and the area was sufficiently remote and wild enough for me to enjoy duck and rabbit hunting as well as bayou and bay fishing.

Today, the area where the camp house stood is now part of the city's municipal golf course and is, of course, within the city limits. Sydnor's Bayou, which used to reward me with trout and redfish, is a body of water filled mostly with scavengers: catfish, piggies and crabs.

Right after the end of World War II my father acquired another camp. This one was located at Anderson's Ways and about five miles more down the island from the first camp. My wife and I stayed there often and spent a lot of time fishing for redfish and speckled trout in adjacent Galveston West Bay.

Fresh out of the army and with no spare change in my pocket, we had to be content to fish from a 16-foot cypress skiff. We kept the skiff pulled out of the water and under the camp to protect it from marine growths. When we planned to go fishing, we would drive down a day early and put the skiff in the water so the wood would "swell up" to close the seams between the bottom planks. I powered the skiff with back muscles and oars. We would row to Confederate Reef a half-mile out in the bay or to South Deer Island, another half-mile beyond the reef. We rarely failed to catch a lot of fish, including speckled trout, at either location.

At the time, there were about 15 camp houses on the mile-long stretch of bayfront known as Anderson's Ways. Today there are close to 100 along this same stretch. Confederate Reef and South Deer Island are still there, but as far as speckled trout fishing is concerned, they are but shadows of a great past.

LONG DISTANCES TO GO

Today if I want to score consistently on speckled trout, or for that matter on any other inshore-waters game fish, I have to travel long distances down the bay. I could never do it now with a heavy skiff and six-foot oars. The first outboard engine I owned was a two-and-a-half-horsepower one-lunger. It could propel me to remote fishing places in Galveston West Bay today, but it would take a good part of the day to get there. The good fishing grounds are no longer just around the corner. They are many miles down the bay and away from civilization, and you need a fast boat to get to those waters and still have a reasonable amount of time to fish.

I have fished all the waters of the greater Galveston bays complex, and as recently as the early 1960s, there were many times when I did not see another fisherman...boater or wader. You don't have that happen now, for on any decent fishing day you can see fishermen in all directions. You never want for company.

FISHING COMPETITION

Most old salts don't mind fishing competition if the people in the other boats know what they are doing. Many old-timers go on the theory that the more bait there is in the water, the longer the fish will hang around. And this is true, but only up to a point. The veterans resent people who rush up at full speed and make all kinds of noise that spook fish. I have some friends who, when they hook a fish and see a boat approaching, do all sorts of things to discourage the competition from staying in the area. When I hook a fish and see a boat approaching, I stick the tip of my rod in the water to keep them from seeing the bend and then pretend as though nothing is happening.

I know one crusty character who detests competition and company. He, too, sticks his rod in the water and acts as if nothing is happening. If the other boaters persist in coming close to check out the action, he will give them some shocking action ... he'll stand up in the boat and relieve himself right over the side. I have seen him do this at least a dozen times, and it never fails to discourage intruders.

The point is that today there is terrific competition for fish, all

Most Gulf coast states have minimum size and bag limits in effect for speckled trout and other saltwater species. Most of those regulations were initiated in the 1970s, and many have been modified since, in an effort to counter increasing pressure on a limited resource. (photo by Larry Bozka)

fish, not just speckled trout. That competition is only going to increase in the years to come.

BAG AND SIZE LIMITS

Most Gulf coast states have minimum size limits and/or bag and possession limits on speckled trout. Most of the regulations were established in the 1970s. Prior to that, about the only regulation was the stipulation that one had to possess a valid fishing license, and even there the requirement of a license to fish in salt water was a late-comer. Prior to 1960, fishing in the salt water of Gulf coast states was free, as long as one was a resident of the state.

The minimum size limit for speckled trout along the Gulf coast ranges from 12 to 14 inches. There had been size limits for years for commercial fishermen; it was in the fall of 1978 when a minimum length of 12 inches was adopted for sport fishing in Texas waters. That was the first for this fish along the Gulf coast. At this writing, the speck's minimum length in Texas waters is 14 inches. Bag limits along the Gulf coast for speckled trout range from 10 per day and 20 in possession to 50 fish, all species in the aggregate, per day.

These are regulations fishermen can live with unless they are out-and-out game hogs. It is just regrettable that the limits came as late as they did. Most sport fishermen who are truly concerned with the future of speckled trout fishing along the Gulf coast would have accepted these limits 10 years earlier, had they known then what they know today.

BREEDING GROUNDS

Fishing pressure on speckled trout has increased many times over the last decade, and there is no doubt the pressure will continue to mount in the years to come. The increased fishing pressure, however, is not the only reason speckled trout need protection.

Fish populations cannot increase or even remain constant when breeding and nursery grounds are disturbed. These grounds have been taking a beating along the Gulf coast and they are far less today than they were decades ago. The bays are still there, but alterations within the bay systems, along the shorelines and on the watersheds that drain into the bay systems, have depleted the breeding and nursery areas.

New ship channels, the dredging of shell, oil exploration and subsequent development, and waterfront housing and recreational additions have altered the ecology of almost every saltwater bay along the Gulf coast, and in almost every case changes have meant a loss of fish-supporting waters. This is considered progress in the march of civilization, but it is most unfortunate that in the march of mankind, the ecology and wildlife have to suffer. You cannot really fathom the significance of these changes until the picture is viewed over a period of time.

Some people consider the dredging of channels as improvements for fishing. This is true if the channels provide bay waters with close ties to the Gulf of Mexico, or if they permit a flushing action in nearly landlocked bays and saltwater lakes. In some cases the channels have improved fishing by making the inland waters more stable in saline content. This is fine.

But channels can be destructive, too. When they slice across flats and marshes, they often deflect currents and the water flow so drastically they impair or destroy adjacent breeding and nursery grounds. When adjacent to or part of industrial ship channels, their dredging can also. I unearth and disperse extremely toxic heavy metals and other harmful substances. The obvious results are polluted bay systems and poisoned oyster reefs.

LOSSES TO POLLUTION

Pollution has taken its toll, and a good example is Offatts Bayou in Galveston. This bayou, which is now in the city limits, years ago had one of the choicest oyster reefs on the entire upper Texas Coast. The bayou itself was nationally known for excellent winter fishing for speckled trout and redfish, and back in the late 1940s and through the mid-1950s, I did feature articles on Offatts Bayou speckled trout fishing for eight national magazines.

Today, the bayou is surrounded by private homes and light industry. Long Reef is dead, no longer producing marketable oysters. There are still a few trout runs each winter, but they are feeble when compared with those of yesteryear.

During the winters of the decades from the 1930s through the 1950s, it was not uncommon to see hundreds of fishermen in the bayou every weekend. A trip would be a poor one if a fisherman failed to catch two or three dozen specks with at least one five-pounder in the lot. In the winters of the last two decades, a good catch would be a 10-fish limit. You don't see several hundred

Fishermen who are truly concerned about the future of our coastal finfish resources would do well to join the Gulf Coast Conservation Association (GCCA). Founded in Houston, Texas, this sportsmen's group has made quantum strides toward protecting game fish species from overharvest. For information, call 713/626-GCCA. (photo by Larry Bozka)

people fishing the bayou on winter weekends any more. The number is closer to a couple of dozen or so.

PROTECTIVE REGULATIONS

There are varying degrees of protection for Gulf coast bays. Most cover the means and methods of taking fish, and they are aimed at all game fish, not just speckled trout.

Most of the regulations pertain to nets and trotlines. A few Gulf coast bays are closed to all types of nets except those used exclusively for catching bait. The states also set seasons and regulations for the commercial taking of bait. As a result of the netting restrictions, there have been frequent cries from commercial fishermen that the ''sports'' (sport fishermen) are trying to put them out of business. Many who complain overlook the fact that the regulations are to insure a future resource of shrimp and fish, and if the supply is allowed to be over-harvested, some of the malcontents may find themselves digging ditches instead of fishing for a living.

Occasionally a combination of circumstances can put undue stress on what the environment can support. This occurred in Texas in the winter of 1978, when in January and February, an estimated quarter-million pounds of speckled trout and redfish were picked up in shrimp trawls in Trinity Bay. The fish were sluggish from the extreme cold, and in their torpid state they were unable to swim fast enough to escape the trawls. It was legal because the bay was open to shrimp trawling at the time. The loss of fish, however, was so great that speckled trout fishing was poor throughout the entire greater Galveston bays complex for the remainder of 1978. Regulations were passed in the next state legislative session to prohibit such massive net harvests from happening again.

Actually, shrimp trawling only occasionally makes serious inroads into the finfish populations, because most game fish are able to swim faster than the nets are dragged. The netting operations that are a constant cause of fish depletion, especially speckled trout and redfish, are the set nets, gill nets and trammel nets that are staked in bays and across the mouths of small bayous and coves. In almost every instance, the netting operations are illegal. State conservation officers keep a never-ending campaign going to minimize illegal netting, but because the warden forces are small, a lot of illegal netters escape and continue to operate.

The future of speckled trout fishing in Gulf coast waters is indeed something to ponder. I have seen it change a lot in the last 50 years. If the downward slide continues, we may not have much speckled trout fishing in the decades to come. But then, why should I worry? At my age, I can't realistically expect more than a decade or two to go.

But I do worry, because it just so happens I have children and grandchildren, and I would like for them to enjoy some of what I have enjoyed in my lifetime. **BB**

AFTERWORD

The production of a book traditionally demands the talents of a number of people who work "behind the scenes." This book is no exception.

The publisher would like to thank the following folks for the part they played in developing the finished product.

John Hillenbrand, art director of Horseman magazine, spent many a late night behind a desktop publishing system getting this book in shape for the printer. John not only designed the layout, chose the type faces and positioned the art; he also played a major role in the creative development of our print advertising campaign.

We contemplated the look of the front cover, and the advertising, for a long time, and it was ultimately the pen of Friendswood, Texas artist Mark Mantell that gave us the touch we needed. A frequent contributor of paintings to conservation groups, Mantell is a rising star in the world of artists who have selected the Gulf Coast and its striking beauty as their chosen genre.

Barbara Robertson, former managing editor of Texas Fisherman and another Friendswood resident, did much of the preliminary research for production as well as the initial pre-editing and typesetting of the copy.

My wife, Mary, not only provided support throughout this entire venture, but did so at the expense of numerous weekends that otherwise would have been family outings. Ditto for my five-year-old son, Jimmy, to whom I owe at least five dozen backyard baseball sessions.

And finally, a sincere word of thanks to the hundreds of thousands of saltwater fishermen along the entire Gulf Coast who have made it possible for people like A.C. Becker, Jr. and me to make a career out of outdoor writing, photography and publishing.

It does, after all, beat working for a living.

Larry Bozka   Houston, Texas

INDEX

OTHER BOOKS BY A.C. BECKER, JR.

Waterfowl in the marshes
(A.S. Barnes, 1969)

Gulf Coast Fishing
(A.S. Barnes, 1970)

Lure Fishing
(A.S. Barnes, 1970)

Big Red/Channel Bass Fishing
(A.S. Barnes, 1972)

Game and Bird Calling
(A.S. Barnes, 1972)

Decoying Waterfowl
(A.S. Barnes, 1973)

Fishing the Texas Coast
(Cordovan Corp., 1975,
Second printing June, 1981)

Texas Saltwater Big Three
(Cordovan Corp., 1976,
Revised edition, 1976)

The Complete Book of Fishing
(A.S. Barnes, 1977)